kingdom.

created to create

Unless otherwise stated, all scripture quotations are from the English Standard Version of the Bible.

Scripture quotations are from the ESV® Bible (The Holy Bible, English Standard Version®), copyright © 2001 by Crossway, a publishing ministry of Good News Publishers. Used by permission.

Scriptures marked KJV are taken from the KING JAMES VERSION (KJV): KING JAMES VERSION, public domain.

kingdom.

CONTENTS

1. Creativity is in your DNA

2. Witty Inventions

3. Faith to Receive

4. Sow for Harvest

Chapter One

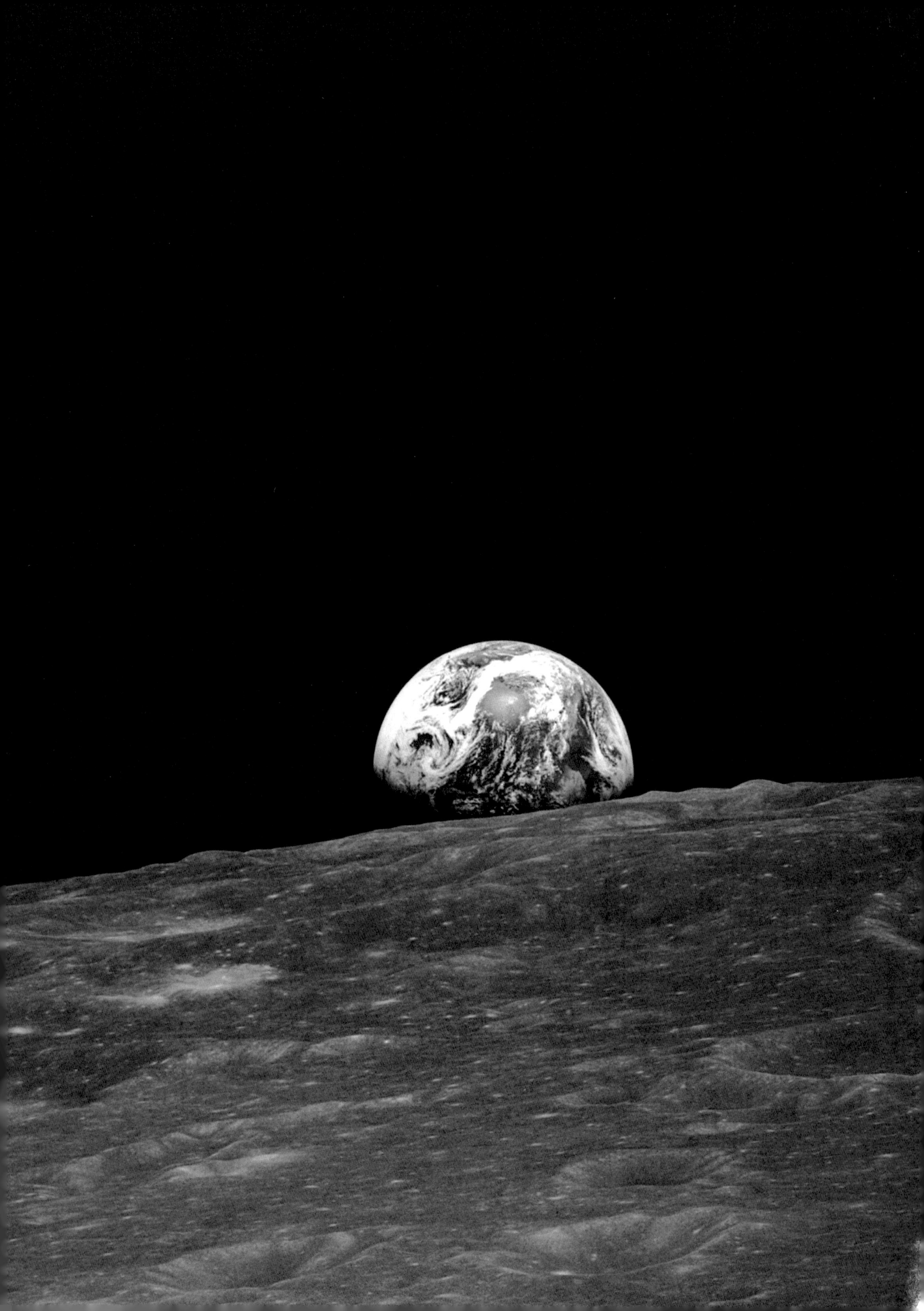

Creativity is in your DNA

"BY FAITH, WE UNDERSTAND THAT THE UNIVERSE WAS CREATED BY THE WORD OF GOD, SO THAT WHAT IS SEEN WAS NOT MADE OUT OF THINGS THAT ARE VISIBLE."
HEBREWS 11:3

God created the angels, heavens, the earth, all living creatures, time, seasons and mankind. Men and women, through their creative genius given to them by God, created everything else. Let that sink in for a moment. Man created everything else. The chair you are sitting in, man created. The computer on which I am typing, man created. The world as we know it, especially in these modern times, is the result of creativity.

It is the result of mankinds' ability to think creatively. One of the greatest weapons against the modern church is not progressive reform, but the lack of creative thinking. If you can think creatively, you can find a solution to any problem.

"THEN GOD SAID, "LET US MAKE MAN IN OUR IMAGE, AFTER OUR LIKENESS.""
GENESIS 1:26

What does it mean to be made in the likeness of God? Many scholars have debated this point over the years, but I feel the simple answer is the truest answer. It is the "God-likeness" within us that empowers us to think and create. Sure, other species can create things like shelters, nests to lay their eggs, burrows for sleeping, etc, but when was the last time you saw a beaver create a chair for sitting or a cup for drinking?

"By faith, we understand that the universe was created by the Word of God, so that what is seen was not made out of things that are visible." Hebrews 11:3

It is the God likeness within us that allows us to take what is not seen, and make it

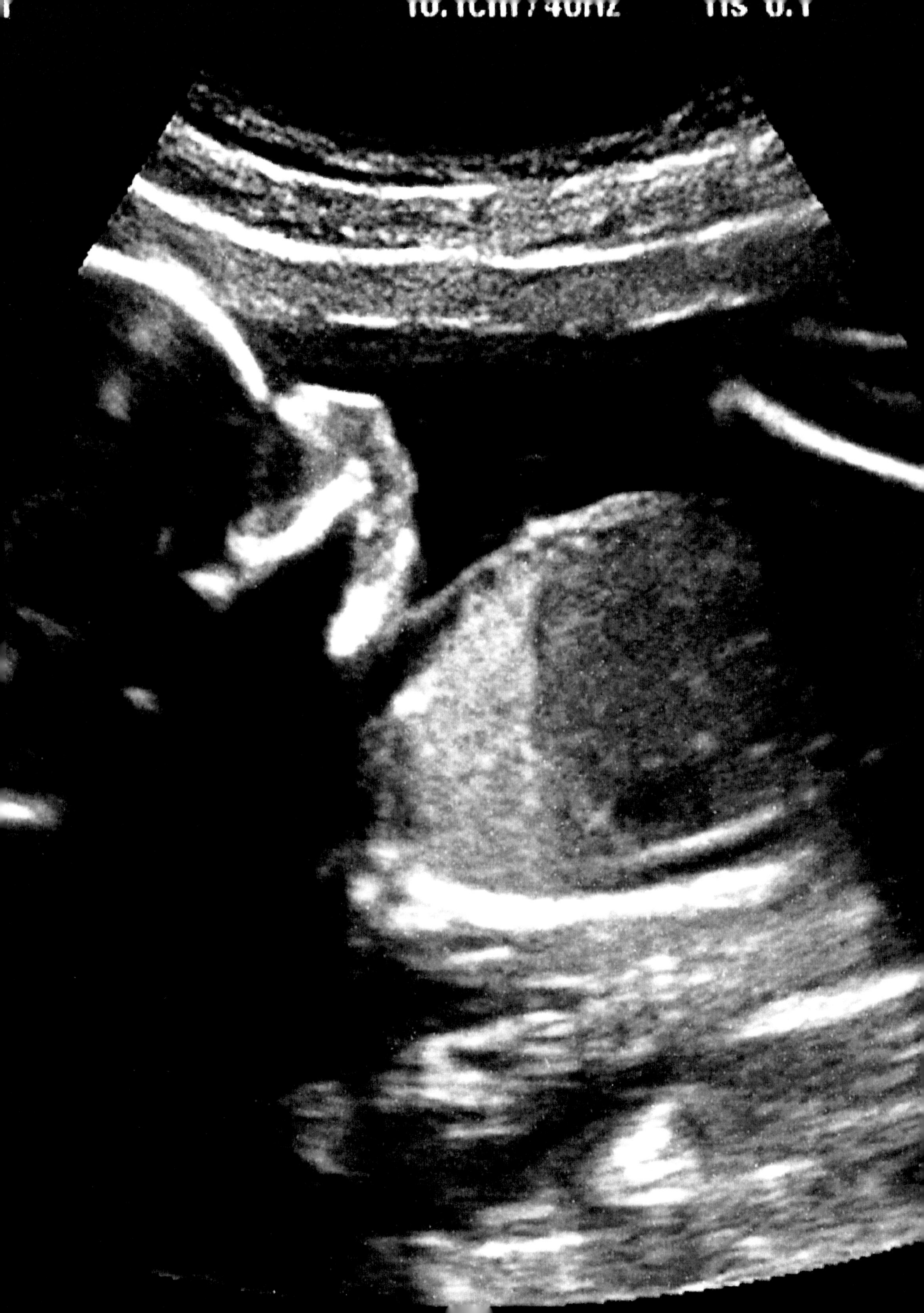

seen. According to Hebrews 11:3, that is exactly how God created the entire universe. Another notable observation of that verse is that the universe was created by the "word" of God. The Greek word in this passage is the word, "rhema". If you run in any prophetic circles, you know the rhema word of God is the "now" word of God; the word God is currently speaking.

> ### "SO, FAITH COMES FROM HEARING, AND HEARING THROUGH THE WORD OF CHRIST."
> ### ROMANS 10:17

We see here that the word, "rhema", is used in Romans 10:17. Faith comes from hearing the "now" spoken word of God, so unless faith is ceasing; the rhema word of God will never cease. Not only is God still speaking, but He is speaking to His children and giving them creative solutions to the world problems today. God created the entire universe with His words, and we create in the same way.

> ### "FROM THE FRUIT OF A MAN'S MOUTH, HIS STOMACH IS SATISFIED;
> ### HE IS SATISFIED BY THE YIELD OF HIS LIPS."
> ### PROVERBS 18:20

Because we are created in the likeness of God, our mouths are always creating something. This is not dependent on what is said; it is simply the principle that when we speak, we create. Period. Psalms 138:2 says that God has even exalted His Word above His name. That means God will not contradict what He has spoken in His Word. He won't bend or break it because of extreme need or lack, nor will He overthrow it because of abundant faith or belief. We must know the Word of God because God, Himself, chooses to fiercely remain faithful to what He has spoken. Even with the purest heart and intent, we can totally miss the full revelation of His Word when we don't understand the principles clearly given to us in the scriptures.

Let's visit Hebrews 11:3 again: "By faith, we understand that the universe was created by the Word of God, so that what is seen was not made out of things that are visible." This tells us that what is currently before us was not simply made from what was already being seen, but it was seen before it was fully made. So, our creative ideas, solutions, and advancements do not come from what is already seen, but what is not yet seen. What is this unseen realm? What is this unseen place in which we draw these manifestations?

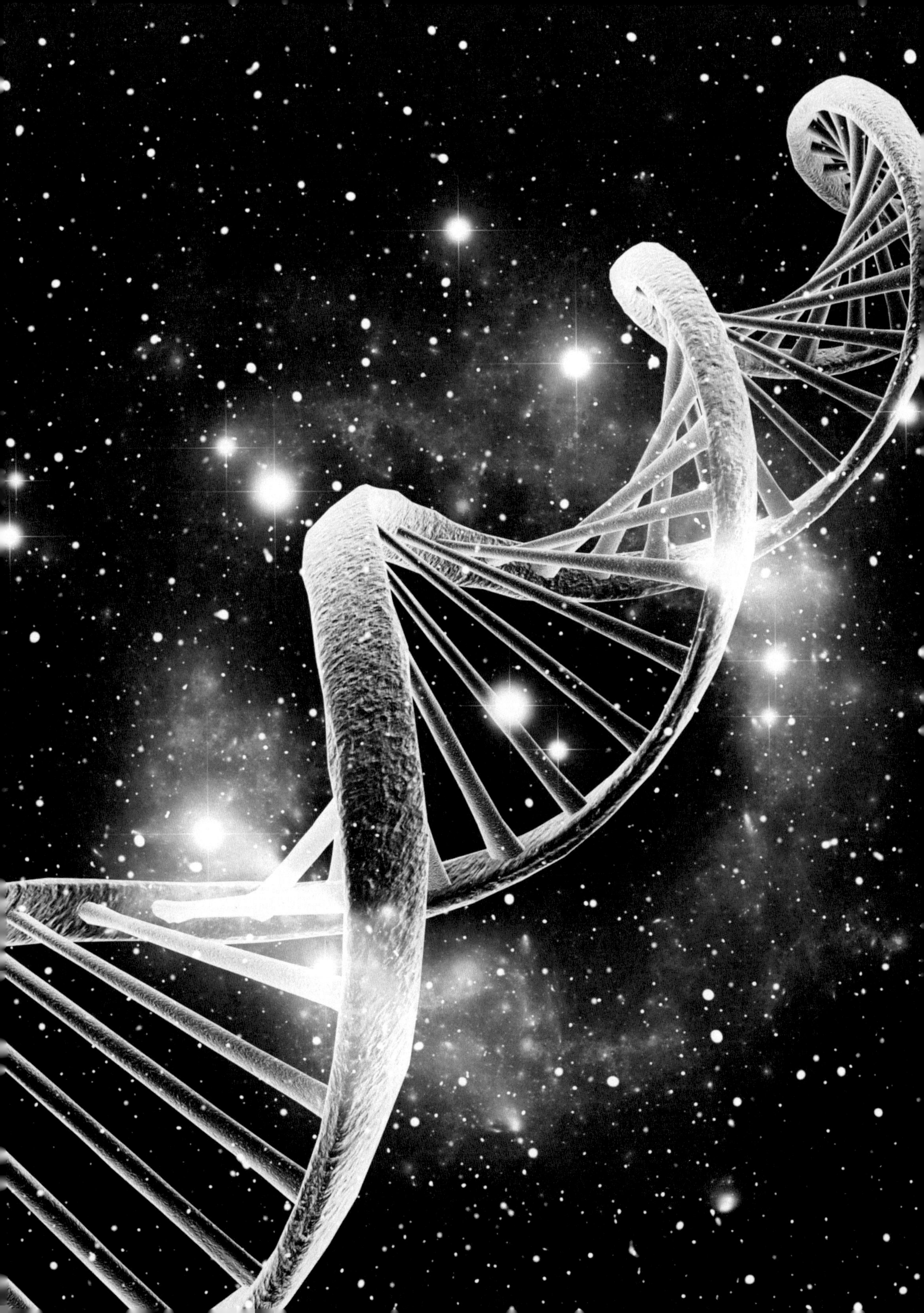

I would submit to you it is the unseen realm of thought. Have you ever envisioned a thought? Have you ever heard another person think while they sat quietly pondering an idea? No. Thoughts are not seen until word and action are partnered with them to cause the thought to become a manifestation in our hand. The ink pen was, first, a thought. The toilet was, first, a thought...thank God for that one! Smart phones were also, once, a thought.

The conception stage of any product, service, business, solution, idea, etc, is a thought. The thought is, then, nurtured or aborted, and it's eventually birthed or disregarded. This is why it is so critical to our human existence to have a space to think and focus. We were created to create. We were not created to simply work and die. We were put here on this earth for innovation, expressive individual creativity, and to implement God's creative genius on the earth.

Do you notice that we do not see or hear of God giving Adam the tools he needed to work the garden as he was instructed in Genesis 2:15? We do not see an hour-by-hour itinerary or instruction manual on how Adam should have worked the garden. Why not? God knew the creative genius He had downloaded into Adam, and I would submit to you that God is excited and eager to see His creative expression working through us. Consider how far we have come as an entire race of human beings from the first garden, all the way to how we cultivate produce and food today. Every bit of innovation that has occurred since the Garden of Eden, to when you last purchased a bag of apples at Wal-Mart, is because of someone's ability to think creatively.

"FOR AS HE THINKETH IN HIS HEART, SO IS HE."
PROVERBS 23:7, KJV

Creative thinking is a weapon in the hand of those who are skillful in stewarding their thought life. Do you know the difference between a homeless man and a man stewarding a mansion from a place of great wealth? It's the ability to think creatively. You can think your way out of any situation or circumstance. We are literally creating our own existence through thought. Remember: "For as he thinketh in his heart, so is he"! This isn't some new-age concept or a bit of wishful thinking; this is the Word of God.

kingdom.

"Creativity is a weapon."

STYLE.

CLASS.

LUXURY.

"ALL THINGS WERE MADE THROUGH HIM, AND WITHOUT HIM, WAS NOT ANYTHING MADE THAT WAS MADE."
JOHN 1:3

All things were made through Him? How can it be that all things are made through God? How can it be that without Him, not anything was made? We look around at this modern world, and we see plenty that we would quickly deem as "not created by God." Yet, John 1:3 tells us that not a single thing can be created without God. How is this so? God gave us the ability to think creatively. The ability to think is the God-likeness within all of us, whether a Christian or not; therefore, everything that was thought and created was created by God.

"ON THE GLORIOUS SPLENDOR OF YOUR MAJESTY, AND ON YOUR WONDROUS WORKS, I WILL MEDITATE."
PSALMS 145:5

Consider all that God has done and all that He has created for us to enjoy. Consider the vivid colors that wrap our world in a cloak of beauty. The yellow sun and its vibrant light. The bursting blooms in spring. The wave of a flickering fire as it dances. The swaying of the trees in the wind we cannot see. His wondrous works invoke a sense of creativity and imagination. Have you ever pondered the angels described in the scriptures or given attention to the animals of the world? What intricate details! What an imagination!

We have that very creative genius within us! Dr. Cindy Trimm said something to the effect of, "If your attempt is to think outside the box, then the box is still your reference point, which means you have truly never been liberated from the box." That statement blew my mind when I first read it, and honestly, it is still continuing to blow my mind, even now. I desire to create, independent of the box the worlds' culture has set before me. I desire to meditate on the glorious splendor of His majesty. I desire to create freely, without man-made boundaries. Creativity is in your DNA. What will you create today?

MY NOTES

MY NOTES

MY NOTES

MY NOTES

MY NOTES

MY NOTES

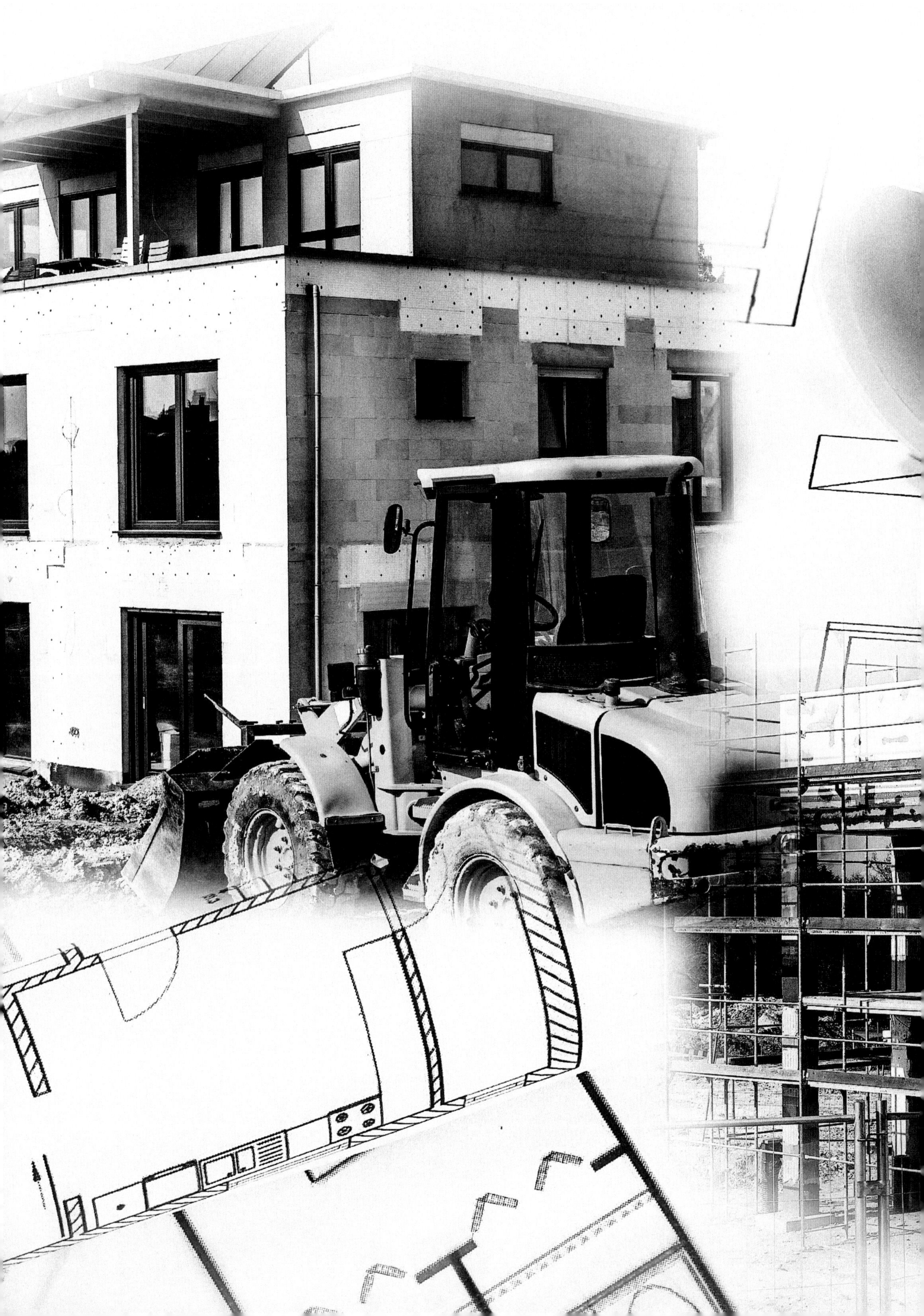

Chapter Two

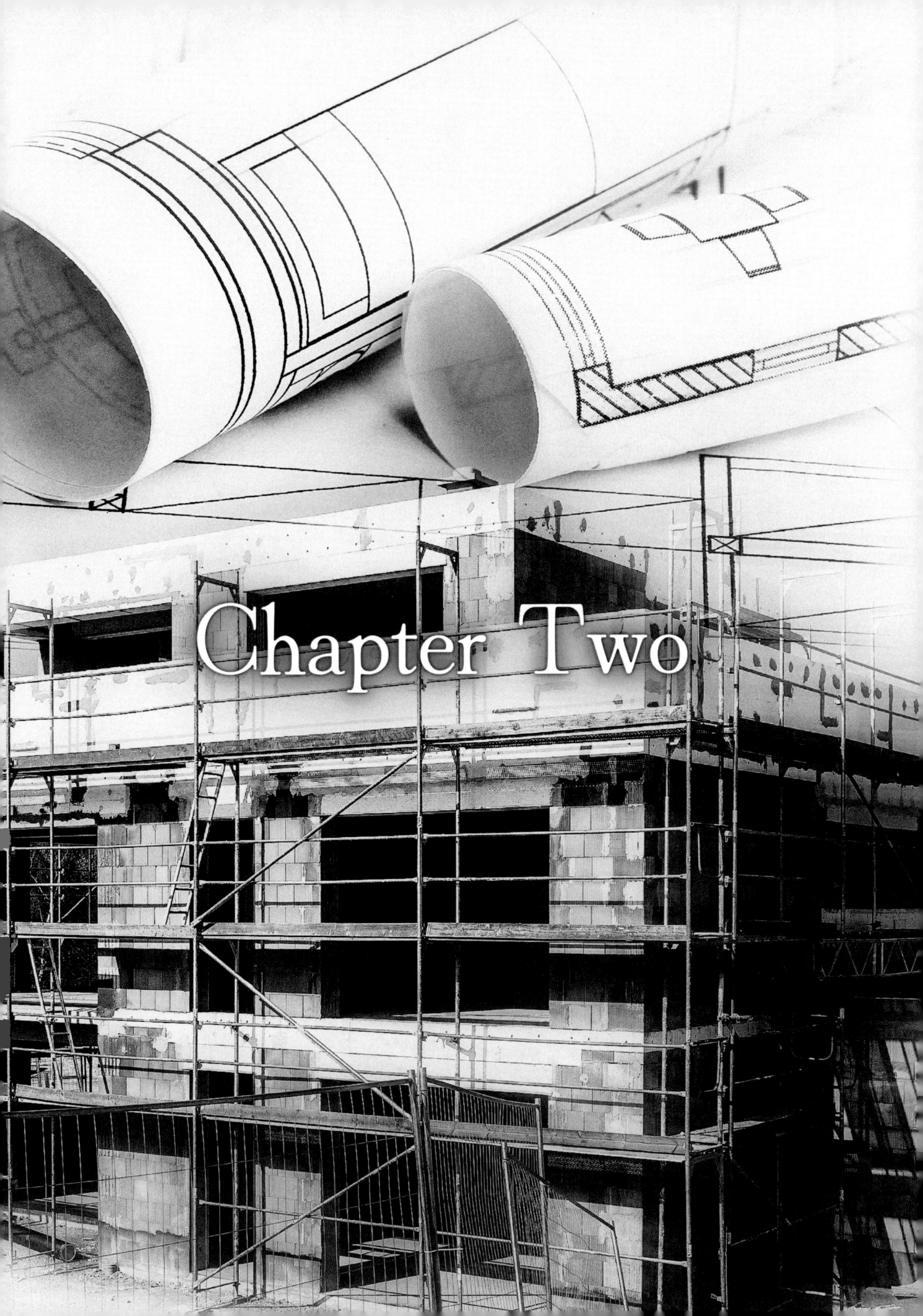

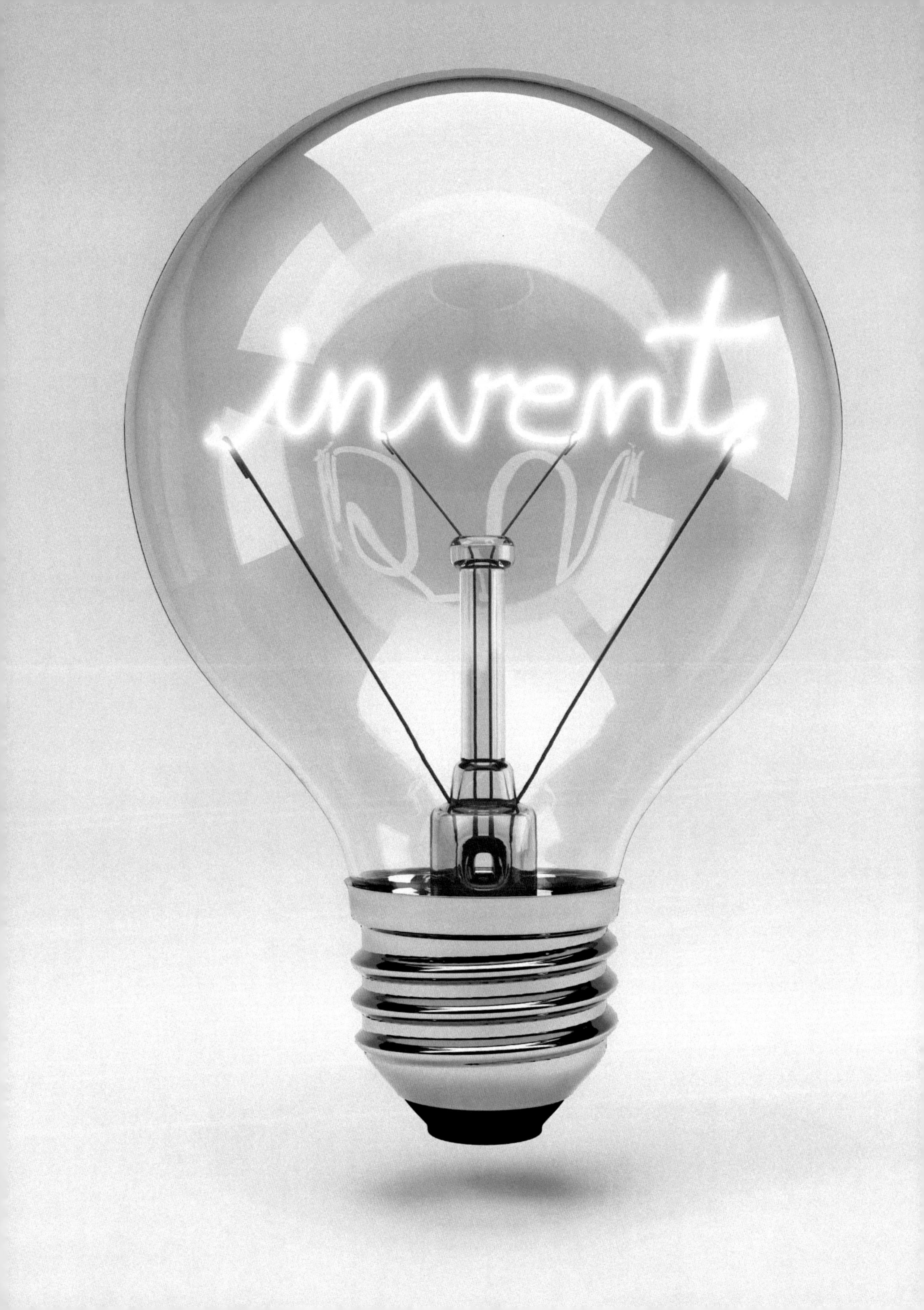
invent

Witty Inventions

"I, WISDOM, DWELL WITH PRUDENCE, AND FIND OUT KNOWLEDGE OF WITTY INVENTIONS."
PROVERBS 8:12

Witty inventions are all around us, and we enjoy the luxuries of them every day. Sure, it is easy to spot the big ones, such as transportation and technology, but our entire lives are dependent on the use of other peoples' witty inventions; even down to a seemingly simple can of green beans. So, then, why not have a few witty inventions of your own?

The truth is that most people don't really believe in their own ability to think or create. They end up relying on others' abilities. Most people have bought into the idea of working an 8a-5p schedule for the youthful years of their life, saving for retirement, and hopefully getting to enjoy the later years of their life, provided that they don't die too early. Our current mode of living is somehow the most advanced and innovative that it has ever been, yet also deeply flawed.

For example, the typical retirement age is 65. According to the 2020 report from the CDC, the average lifespan is 73 years of age; the initial estimated lifespan was 78 years of age, but has dropped by 5 years due to the Covid-19 virus. So, we work all our lives to pay for a home that we are almost never in and raise children that we almost never see, all for hoping to enjoy 8 years of our lives in the way we want. What!? Just a quick Google search will tell you that 1% of the population has anywhere from 43%-70% of the global wealth, depending on the study given. Are we not the children of God?

Over the years, the church has stepped out of most spheres of influence, even demonizing those in the church who spread messages of going back into the world to change it, rather than sitting in prayer closets, waiting for something to happen. Sadly, it has taught the rest of us to do the same. We are beginning to see devout Christans penetrating the core of society again, but there are certainly many more seats at the table. Could it be that our holy stance against world industries is why the world is in its current condition?

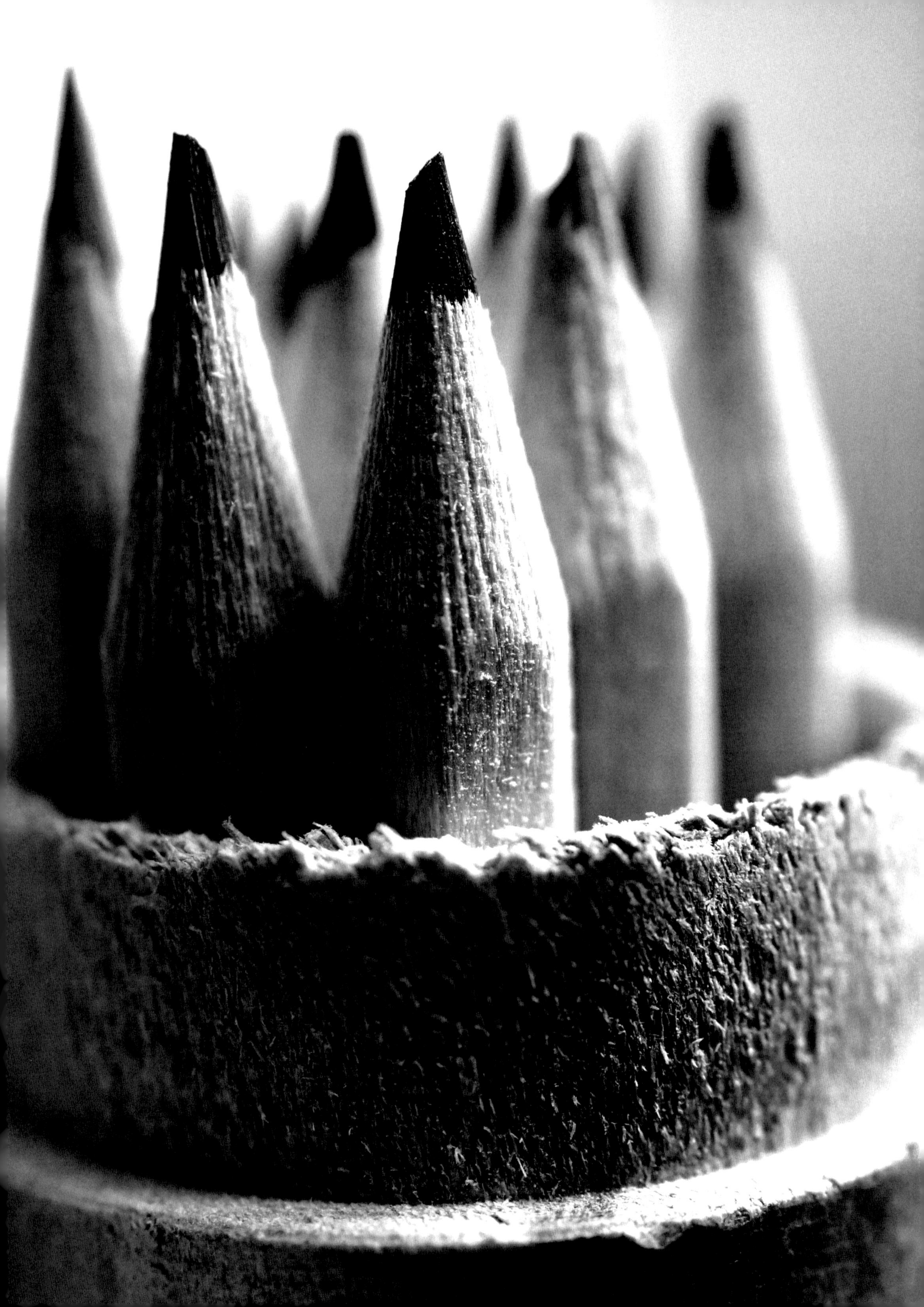

No matter your viewpoint, the rapture doctrine is a rather new doctrine, dating back to about the 1830s. With the introduction of this doctrine, many Christians have adopted an escapist mentality. We are waiting to "be saved" while there is a world around us that needs saving. With this thought in tow, some (and usually the more radical) Christians live their lives completely separated from society as a whole. It certainly insinuates that some have more faith in the darkness getting on them than the light they carry getting on and in the society in which they function.

I am a vocational minister, and in the early years of my ministry, I had many business opportunities to bring my family wealth and increase (much as I do now), yet I was advised by well-meaning church leaders that a pastor cannot be in ministry and business. Why? That is silly. Paul was, both, a minister and business owner (Acts 18). Likewise, most of the apostles called by Jesus were business owners. We forget that Peter was married, according to Luke 4:38-40. Do we believe that Jesus called Peter away from his family and left them with no provision or means? I don't believe so. 1 Timothy 5:8 says that if a man does not provide for his own household, he has denied the faith, and he is worse than an unbeliever. I would submit to you that Peter had an abundance to care for his family while he did the work of the ministry.

This idea that Christian's cannot participate in society or wealth is a demonic plot from hell. Each person is called to the level of concentration that they're called to, but understand that the scripture tells all of us to make disciples as we go (Matthew 28:19). As we go to work in the medical field, we are to make disciples. As we go to work as a YouTube influencer, we are to make disciples. As we go to work as a shopping clerk at Target, we are to make disciples.

It is time the church begins looking at this life we have been given with a new creative lens and perspective. What witty inventions are on the inside of you? For which problems do you have a solution? How much more of an impact could you make if you had the resources needed to be a blessing? We say cliches like, "I am blessed to be a blessing!", yet many are struggling in debt and living paycheck to paycheck. In 2 Corinthians 8:13, the apostle, Paul, said that we should not ease the burden of another by means of burdening ourselves. Scripture also tells us to leave the "edges of our fields" for the poor and needy in Leviticus 23:22. What edges do you have left over? The leftovers from our abundance should be designated for alms and meeting needs. We will discuss that more in the last chapter.

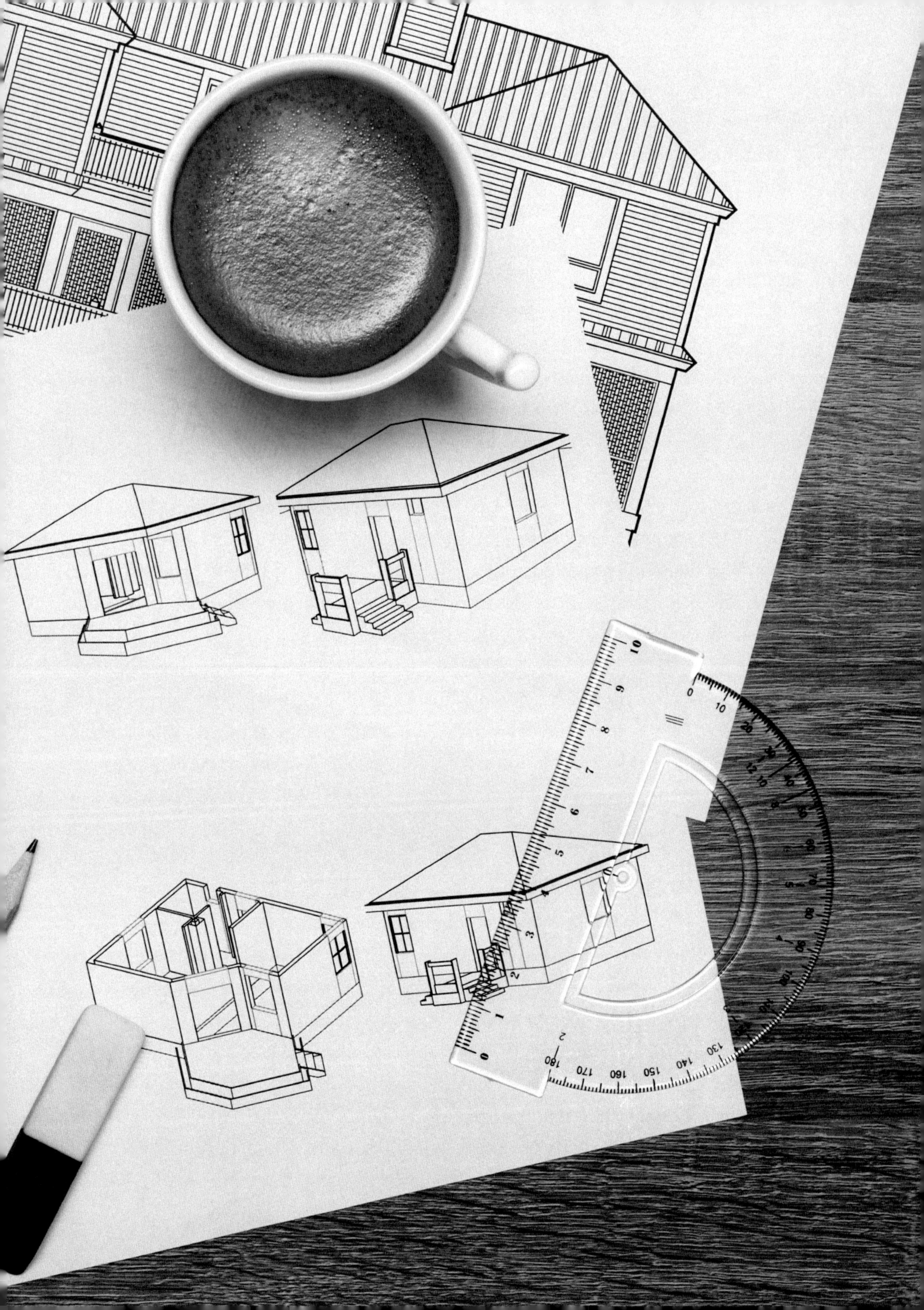

Do you see my point, though? This mindset of demonizing money, wealth, business, and the various spheres of influence in society, is truthfully one of complete fear. I resonate with the words of the apostle, Paul, and I remember just how deep the pit I was brought out of was. No amount of success or influence will take me from my Jesus. He received the glory when I had nothing, and He will receive the glory when I have everything.

> **"FOR I AM CONVINCED THAT NEITHER DEATH, NOR LIFE, NOR ANGELS, NOR PRINCIPALITIES, NOR THINGS PRESENT, NOR THINGS TO COME, NOR POWERS, NOR HEIGHT, NOR DEPTH, NOR ANY OTHER CREATED THING, WILL BE ABLE TO SEPARATE US FROM THE LOVE OF GOD, WHICH IS IN CHRIST JESUS OUR LORD."**
> **ROMANS 8:38-39**

What witty inventions are on the inside of you? A great indicator that you may have a solution to a problem is the frustration that rises up within you when a particular thing is done wrong. What makes you most inspired? If all the pressures were off, money was not a concern, etc, what would you do? What would you be? What would you create? God wants to give us witty ideas. His word shows us that, throughout all the ages, He has given men and women witty inventions. Did you know that Einstein discovered the theory of relativity through a dream? He dreamed of cows standing by an electric fence. Both of the cows jumped when they were shocked; however, a farmer was standing on the other side of the fence and saw the cows jump one by one. This dream inspired Einstein that the same event looks different, depending on your viewpoint during the actual event because of the light traveling to your eyes. That is a witty discovery.

Did you know that Fredrick Banting was a scientist that discovered insulin, which is effective in treating diabetes? He discovered this through a series of dreams concerning diabetic dogs and their pancreases. He was awarded a Nobel Prize at the age of 32. Millions of people have had a chance to live because of this discovery. That is a witty invention. Did you know that YouTube was created in 2005 with the simple idea that people would like to share their home videos online? Steve Chen, Chad Hurley, and Jawed Karim are the names of three former employees of PayPal that came together to offer a solution to a problem that few people even realized they had; the inability to

What will you create?

Online Banking
$ 55,678.99
Current Balance
$ 5,678.99
Current Balance
$ 5,678.99
Current Balance
$ 5,678.99
Current Balance
Personal Account
Account Details
Mobile Payment
Personal Loan
Deposites
Bank Visa
12345678
Last Payment 2022-02-20
$ 2,678.99
Transfers
Saving
Seting
Log Out

share videos online. Today, YouTube is worth $19.7 billion. A company that was created 16 years ago is now worth $19.7 billion dollars, and it has completely revolutionized society. Before the creation of YouTube, if you wanted to have a "channel" on a mainstream outlet, you had to be famous. Today, some YouTubers are more famous and more wealthy than Hollywood elites. That is all the result of a witty invention.

The possibilities are endless. The untapped and unseen realm is just waiting to be made visible. How will your life impact society? How will your creativity leave a legacy for years and years to come?

MY NOTES

MY NOTES

MY NOTES

MY NOTES

MY NOTES

MY NOTES

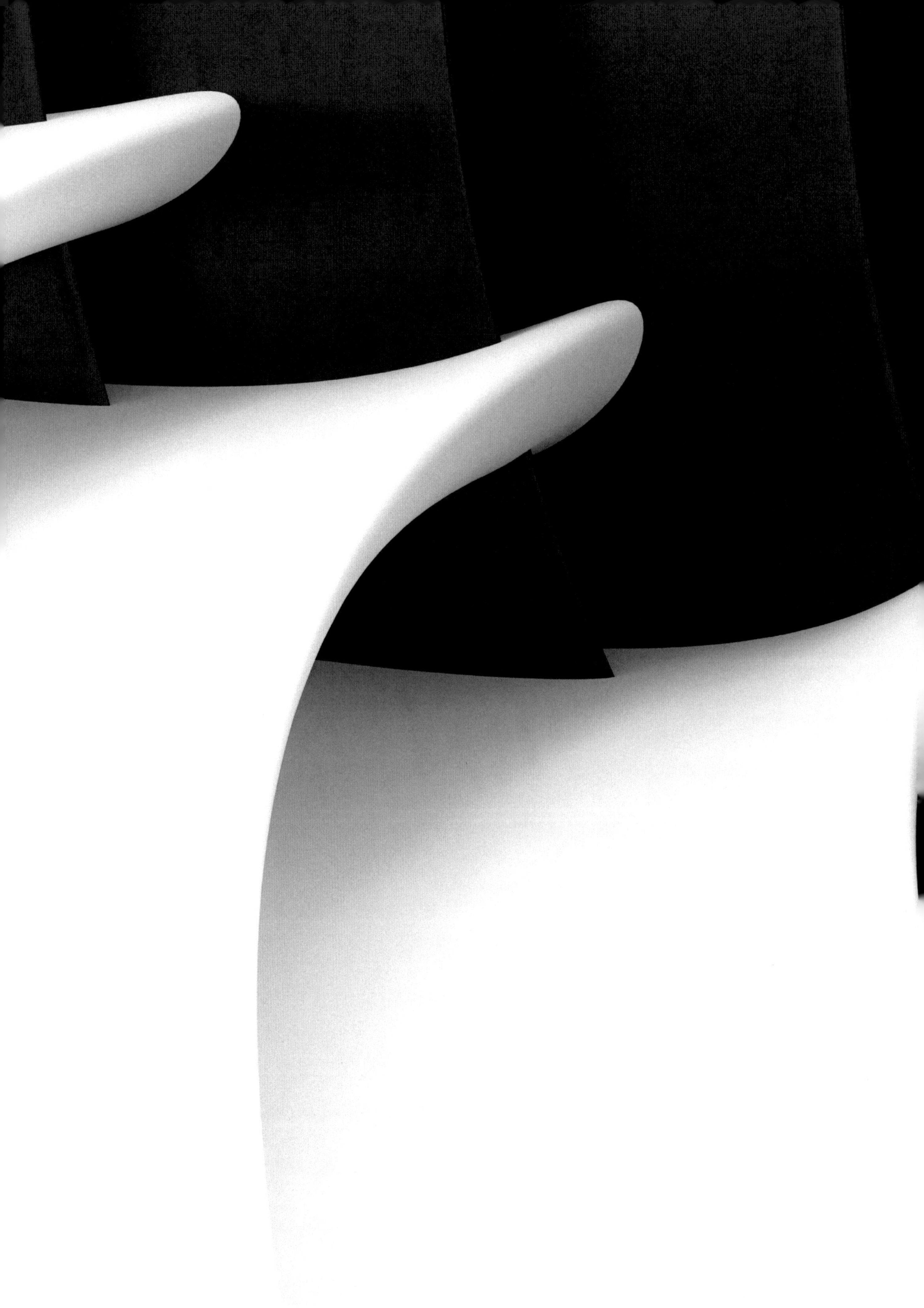

Chapter Three

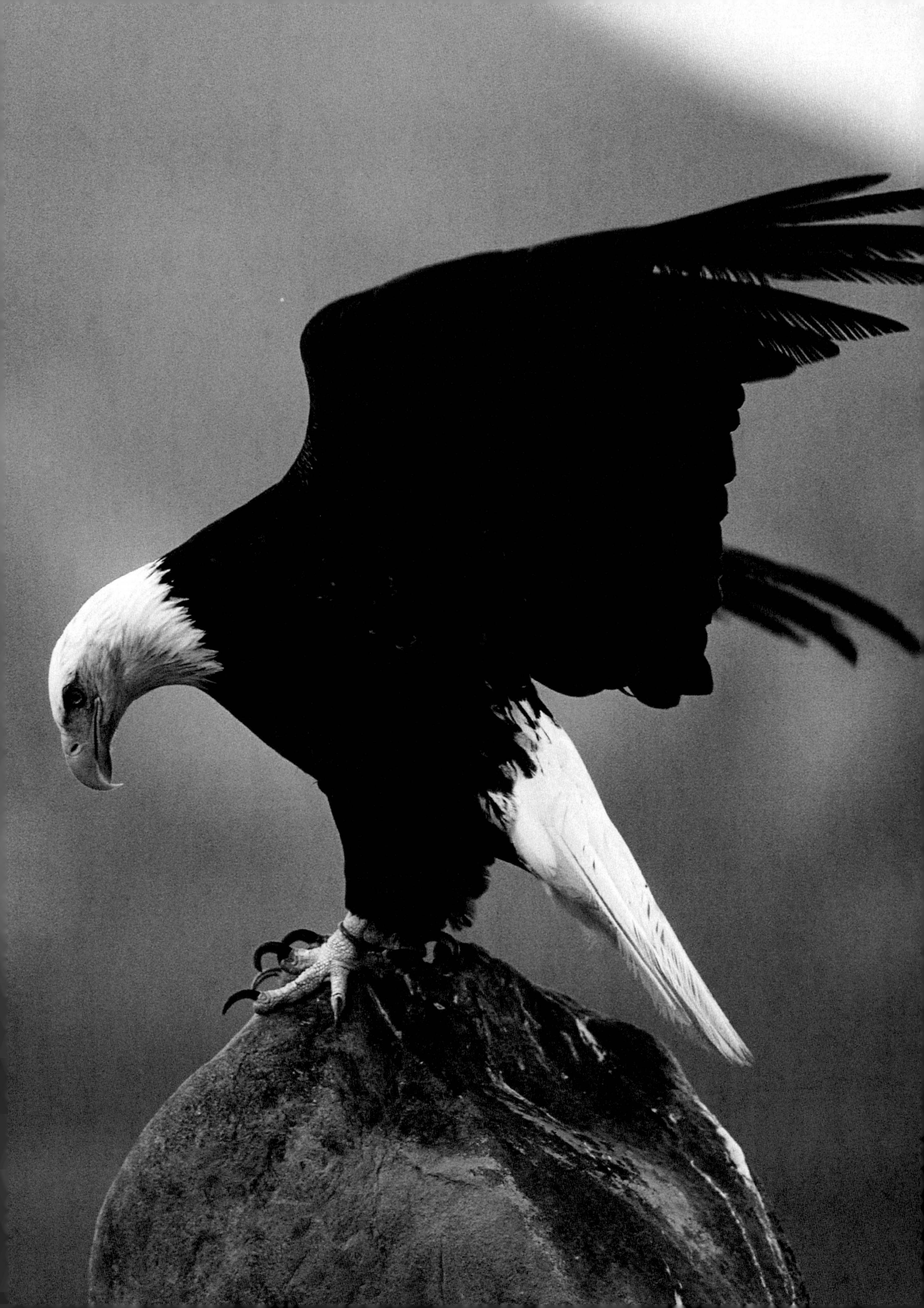

Faith to Receive

"GOD IS NOT A MAN, THAT HE SHOULD LIE; NEITHER THE SON OF MAN, THAT HE SHOULD REPENT: HATH HE SAID, AND SHALL HE NOT DO IT? OR HATH HE SPOKEN, AND SHALL HE NOT MAKE IT GOOD?" NUMBERS 23:19

If God said it, we can believe it, right? Right! Solely focusing on the scriptures we feel best coddle our own viewpoints or make us feel most comfortable, is evidence of not believing God at His full Word. When we do this, we are literally choosing to designate parts of God that we like and dislike. The book that declares Jesus is Lord is the same book that says, in Deuteronomy 8:18, "You shall remember the Lord your God, for it is He who gives you power to get wealth, that He may confirm His covenant that he swore to your fathers, as it is this day." It's right there in His Word. How interesting.

So, we see that a way in which God confirms His covenant with us is through His supernatural empowerment to get wealth. If you talk about this within the modern-day church, you are labeled as a "prosperity preacher". I am not sure why saying that God gives us the ability to have more than enough offends people, but boy, oh boy, it absolutely does! Offended or not, our heart posture does not stop the Word of God from being the Word of God, nor does it nullify the powerful effect of its truth in our lives. It is as though Christians believe that if you have an over-abundance, it must mean someone else is walking in lack. That is such a scarce mentality that produces an apologetic disposition toward being prosperous; we were never meant to carry such a mentality!

I do not have to go without for you to have, nor does my abundance take away from your daily needs being met. As we discussed in the previous chapter, when I have abundance, I can help others in need. Proverbs 13:22 says, "A good man leaves an inheritance to his children's children, but the sinner's wealth is laid up for the righteous." How am I to leave my children and their children an inheritance if all I have is enough to meet my daily needs? Also, consider that, culturally speaking, this scripture was not written in our modern, nuclear-family-unit idea (husband,

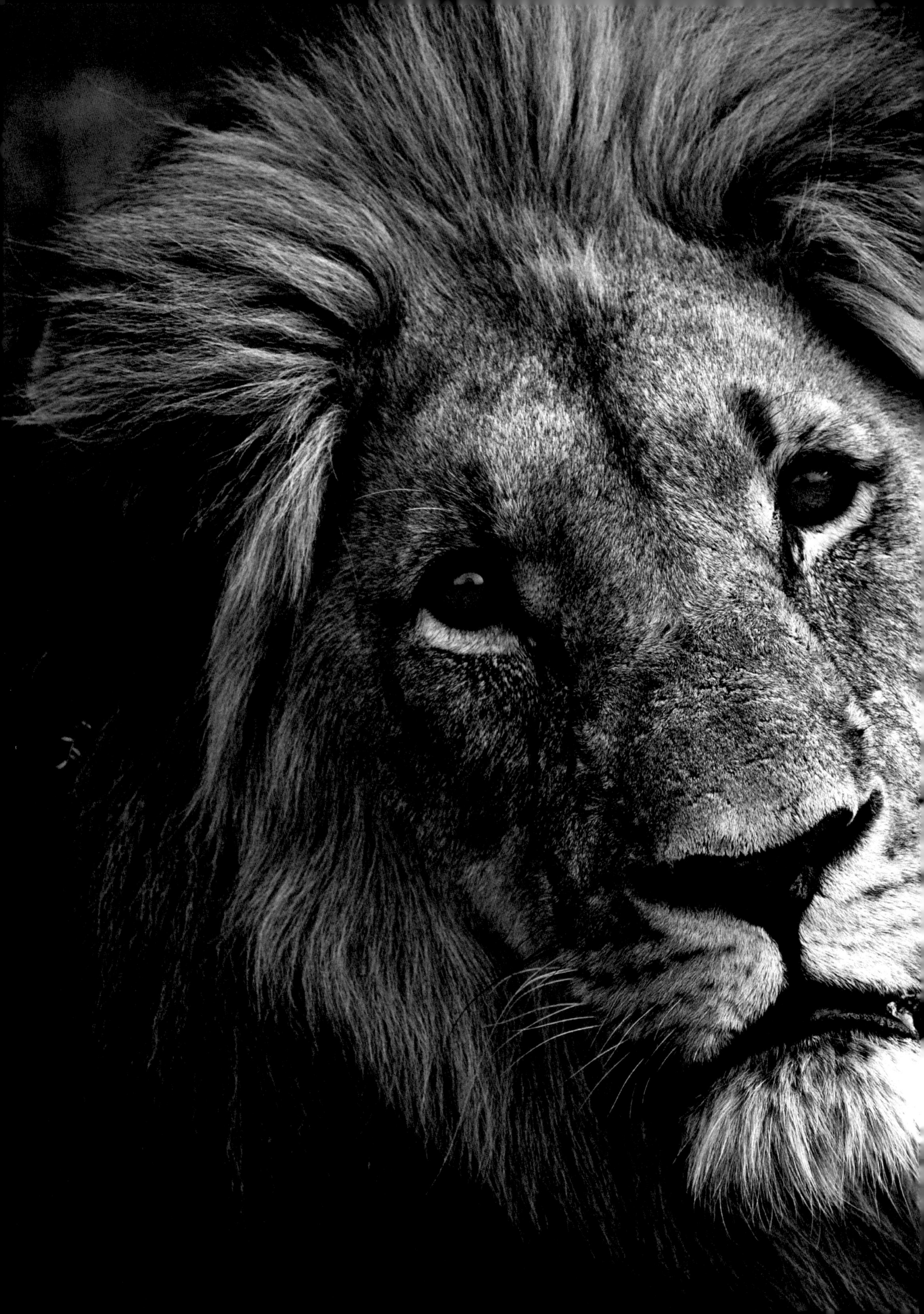

wife, one boy, one girl). They had huge families! Today, we consider the nations of the world, but we often forget that before they were nations, they were families. Scripture says a good man leaves an inheritance for his children and his grandchildren. This implies much more than we might realize at first glance.

If we believe God's promises and the many, many scriptures concerning His heart toward our increase and abundance, we must step into them with faith. A lack of faith in what God has said can stop us from fully stepping into that fullness of what He has given us through His word. Let these promises from God's word encourage you to faith. I even encourage you to grab a sticky note, (which by the way was a very witty invention) and write some of these scriptures down. Put them on your mirror, your office desk, your refrigerator, your workout area, or anywhere else you will see them. The Word of God is effective! When you allow His Word to be a consistent visual reminder, it goes down deep and does what it was created to do. Screenshot the verses and put them as the background on your phone or iPad until you KNOW them in your heart.

"AND MY GOD WILL SUPPLY EVERY NEED OF YOURS ACCORDING TO HIS RICHES IN GLORY IN CHRIST JESUS." PHILIPPIANS 4:19

"THIS BOOK OF THE LAW SHALL NOT DEPART FROM YOUR MOUTH, BUT YOU SHALL MEDITATE ON IT DAY AND NIGHT, SO THAT YOU MAY BE CAREFUL TO DO ACCORDING TO ALL THAT IS WRITTEN IN IT. FOR THEN, YOU WILL MAKE YOUR WAY PROSPEROUS, AND THEN YOU WILL HAVE GOOD SUCCESS." JOSHUA 1:8

"YOU SHALL EAT THE FRUIT OF THE LABOR OF YOUR HANDS; YOU SHALL BE BLESSED, AND IT SHALL BE WELL WITH YOU." PSALMS 128:2

"AND GOD IS ABLE TO MAKE ALL GRACE ABOUND TO YOU, SO THAT HAVING ALL SUFFICIENCY IN ALL THINGS AT ALL TIMES, YOU MAY ABOUND IN EVERY GOOD WORK." 2 CORINTHIANS 9:8

"AND IF YOU FAITHFULLY OBEY THE VOICE OF THE LORD YOUR GOD, BEING CAREFUL TO DO ALL HIS COMMANDMENTS THAT I COMMAND YOU TODAY, THE LORD YOUR GOD WILL SET YOU HIGH ABOVE ALL THE NATIONS OF THE EARTH. AND ALL THESE BLESSINGS SHALL COME UPON YOU AND OVERTAKE YOU, IF YOU OBEY THE VOICE OF THE LORD, YOUR GOD. BLESSED SHALL YOU BE IN THE CITY, AND BLESSED SHALL YOU BE IN THE FIELD. BLESSED SHALL BE THE FRUIT OF YOUR WOMB AND THE FRUIT OF YOUR GROUND AND THE FRUIT OF YOUR CATTLE, THE INCREASE OF YOUR HERDS AND THE YOUNG OF YOUR FLOCK. BLESSED SHALL BE YOUR BASKET AND YOUR KNEADING BOWL." DEUTERONOMY 28:1-6

"THEN I REPLIED TO THEM, 'THE GOD OF HEAVEN WILL MAKE US PROSPER, AND WE HIS SERVANTS WILL ARISE AND BUILD.'" NEHEMIAH 2:20

"THE BLESSING OF THE LORD MAKETH RICH, AND HE ADDS NO SORROW WITH IT."
PROVERBS 10:22

"PRAISE THE LORD! BLESSED IS THE MAN WHO FEARS THE LORD, WHO GREATLY DELIGHTS IN HIS COMMANDMENTS! HIS OFFSPRING WILL BE MIGHTY IN THE LAND; THE GENERATION OF THE UPRIGHT WILL BE BLESSED. WEALTH AND RICHES ARE IN HIS HOUSE, AND HIS RIGHTEOUSNESS ENDURES FOREVER." PSALMS 112:1-3

"OH, TASTE AND SEE THAT THE LORD IS GOOD! BLESSED IS THE MAN WHO TAKES REFUGE IN HIM! OH, FEAR THE LORD, YOU HIS SAINTS, FOR THOSE WHO FEAR HIM HAVE NO LACK! THE YOUNG LIONS SUFFER WANT AND HUNGER; BUT THOSE WHO SEEK THE LORD LACK NO GOOD THING." PSALMS 34:8-10

"THE THIEF COMES ONLY TO STEAL AND KILL AND DESTROY. I CAME THAT THEY MAY HAVE LIFE AND HAVE IT MORE ABUNDANTLY." JOHN 10:10

"JABEZ CALLED UPON THE GOD OF ISRAEL, SAYING, "OH THAT YOU WOULD BLESS ME AND ENLARGE MY BORDER, AND THAT YOUR HAND MIGHT BE WITH ME, AND THAT YOU WOULD KEEP ME FROM HARM SO THAT IT MIGHT NOT BRING ME PAIN!" AND GOD GRANTED WHAT HE ASKED." 1 CHRONICLES 4:10

"A PSALM OF DAVID. THE LORD IS MY SHEPHERD; I SHALL NOT WANT. HE MAKES ME LIE DOWN IN GREEN PASTURES. HE LEADS ME BESIDE STILL WATERS. HE RESTORES MY SOUL. HE LEADS ME IN PATHS OF RIGHTEOUSNESS FOR HIS NAME'S SAKE." PSALMS 23:1-3

"THUS SAYS THE LORD, YOUR REDEEMER, THE HOLY ONE OF ISRAEL: 'I AM THE LORD YOUR GOD, WHO TEACHES YOU TO PROFIT, WHO LEADS YOU IN THE WAY YOU SHOULD GO.'" ISAIAH 48:17

"THE REWARD FOR HUMILITY AND FEAR OF THE LORD IS RICHES AND HONOR AND LIFE."
PROVERBS 22:4

"AND WITHOUT FAITH, IT IS IMPOSSIBLE TO PLEASE HIM, FOR WHOEVER WOULD DRAW NEAR TO GOD MUST BELIEVE THAT HE EXISTS, AND THAT HE REWARDS THOSE WHO SEEK HIM."
HEBREWS 11:6

"AND I WILL MAKE YOU A GREAT NATION, AND I WILL BLESS YOU AND MAKE YOUR NAME GREAT, SO THAT YOU WILL BE A BLESSING. I WILL BLESS THOSE WHO BLESS YOU, AND HE WHO DISHONORS YOU, I WILL CURSE, AND IN YOU ALL THE FAMILIES OF THE EARTH SHALL BE BLESSED." GENESIS 12:2-3

"IF THEY LISTEN AND SERVE HIM, THEY COMPLETE THEIR DAYS IN PROSPERITY, AND THEIR YEARS IN PLEASANTNESS."
JOB 36:11

"AND KEEP THE CHARGE OF THE LORD YOUR GOD, WALKING IN HIS WAYS AND KEEPING HIS STATUTES, HIS COMMANDMENTS, HIS RULES, AND HIS TESTIMONIES, AS IT IS WRITTEN IN THE LAW OF MOSES, THAT YOU MAY PROSPER IN ALL THAT YOU DO AND WHEREVER YOU TURN..."
1 KINGS 2:3

"NOW TO HIM WHO IS ABLE TO DO FAR MORE ABUNDANTLY THAN ALL THAT WE ASK OR THINK, ACCORDING TO THE POWER AT WORK WITHIN US..." EPHESIANS 3:20

"IF YOU ARE WILLING AND OBEDIENT, YOU SHALL EAT THE GOOD OF THE LAND..." ISAIAH 1:19

"GOD SETTLES THE SOLITARY IN A HOME; HE LEADS OUT THE PRISONERS TO PROSPERITY, BUT THE REBELLIOUS DWELL IN A PARCHED LAND." PSALMS 68:6

"THEN YOU SHALL SEE AND BE RADIANT; YOUR HEART SHALL THRILL AND EXULT, BECAUSE THE ABUNDANCE OF THE SEA SHALL BE TURNED TO YOU, THE WEALTH OF THE NATIONS SHALL COME TO YOU." ISAIAH 60:5

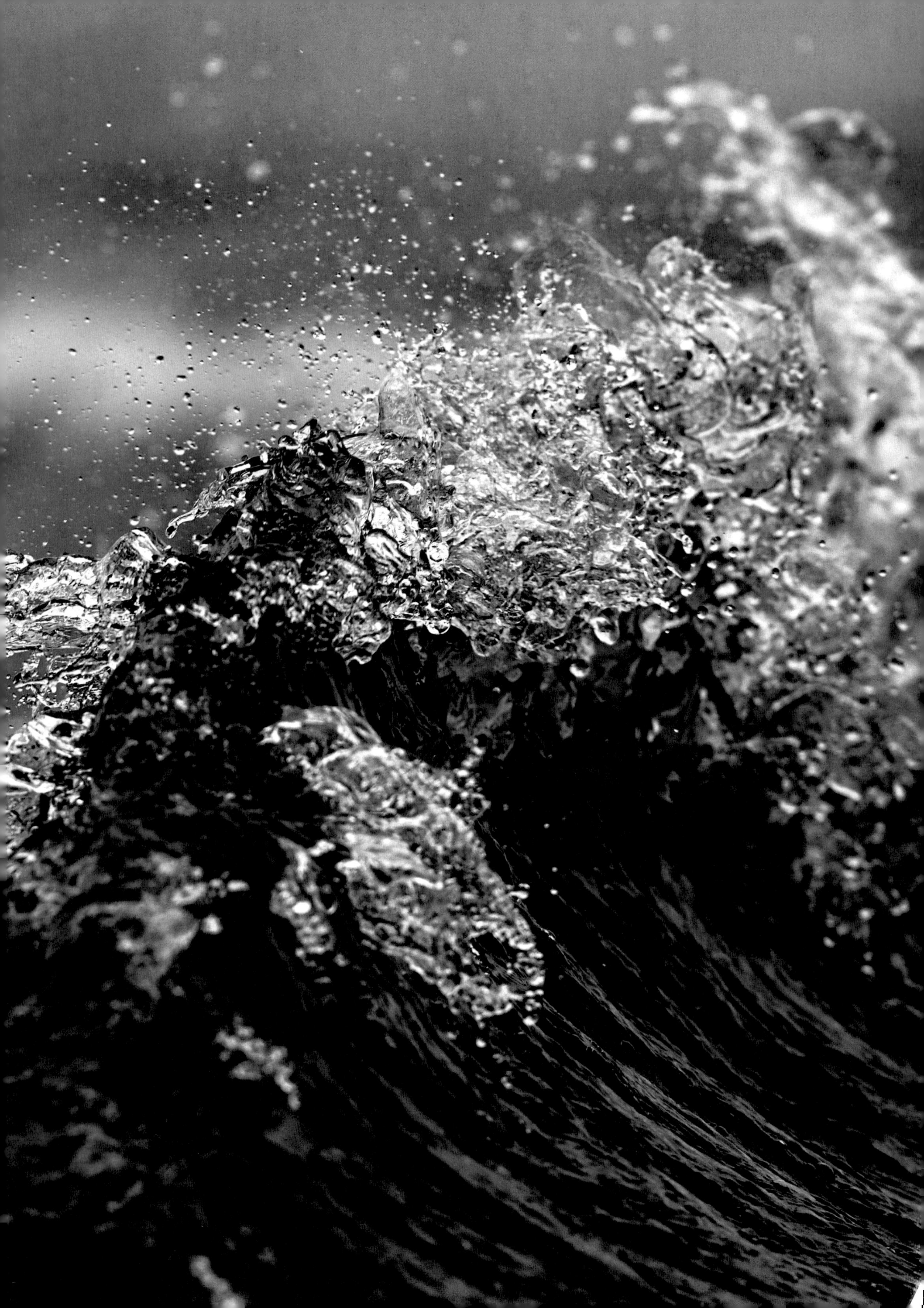

> **"I WILL REBUKE THE DEVOURER FOR YOU, SO THAT IT WILL NOT DESTROY THE FRUITS OF YOUR SOIL, AND YOUR VINE IN THE FIELD SHALL NOT FAIL TO BEAR, SAYS THE LORD OF HOSTS. THEN ALL NATIONS WILL CALL YOU BLESSED, FOR YOU WILL BE A LAND OF DELIGHT, SAYS THE LORD OF HOSTS."**
> **MALACHI 3:11-12**

If we are going to be liberated from the box, think creatively, and step into witty inventions, we must also understand that wealth will be a byproduct of that. Don't be a blessing blocker! I know many of us have teachings that say, "money is the root of all evil", but that is a gross misquoting of the scriptures.

> **"FOR THE LOVE OF MONEY IS A ROOT OF ALL KINDS OF EVIL. IT IS THROUGH THIS CRAVING THAT SOME HAVE WANDERED AWAY FROM THE FAITH AND PIERCED THEMSELVES WITH MANY PANGS."**
> **1 TIMOTHY 6:10**

The love of money is a root of all kinds of evil. The root of all evil is sin, not money. We know there was sin long before currency was a thing. Do you love money, or do you love Jesus? You cannot serve money and Jesus, but you can make money and serve Jesus. The Lord certainly isn't implying that money or the possession of it is evil or has some potential to steal your salvation. The real question is this: Do you possess money, or does money possess you?

When I spoke in the second chapter of how the Church truly needs to be delivered from these types of thinking, this was one of the things in which I was speaking. We have to be liberated from the idea that impacting society, and/or making great wealth while doing so, is something in which God does not approve. If you have followed me or my ministry for any amount of time, you know I lead with transparency. That is just how I do things.

Flowing in my transparent vein, the area of finances is an area in which I desperately needed liberation. I was raised in middle-class America. We weren't extremely wealthy when I was growing up, but we certainly were not poor. I got to enjoy vacations to Disney World, and I enjoyed designer clothing, but I lived a very normal 3-bedroom, 2-

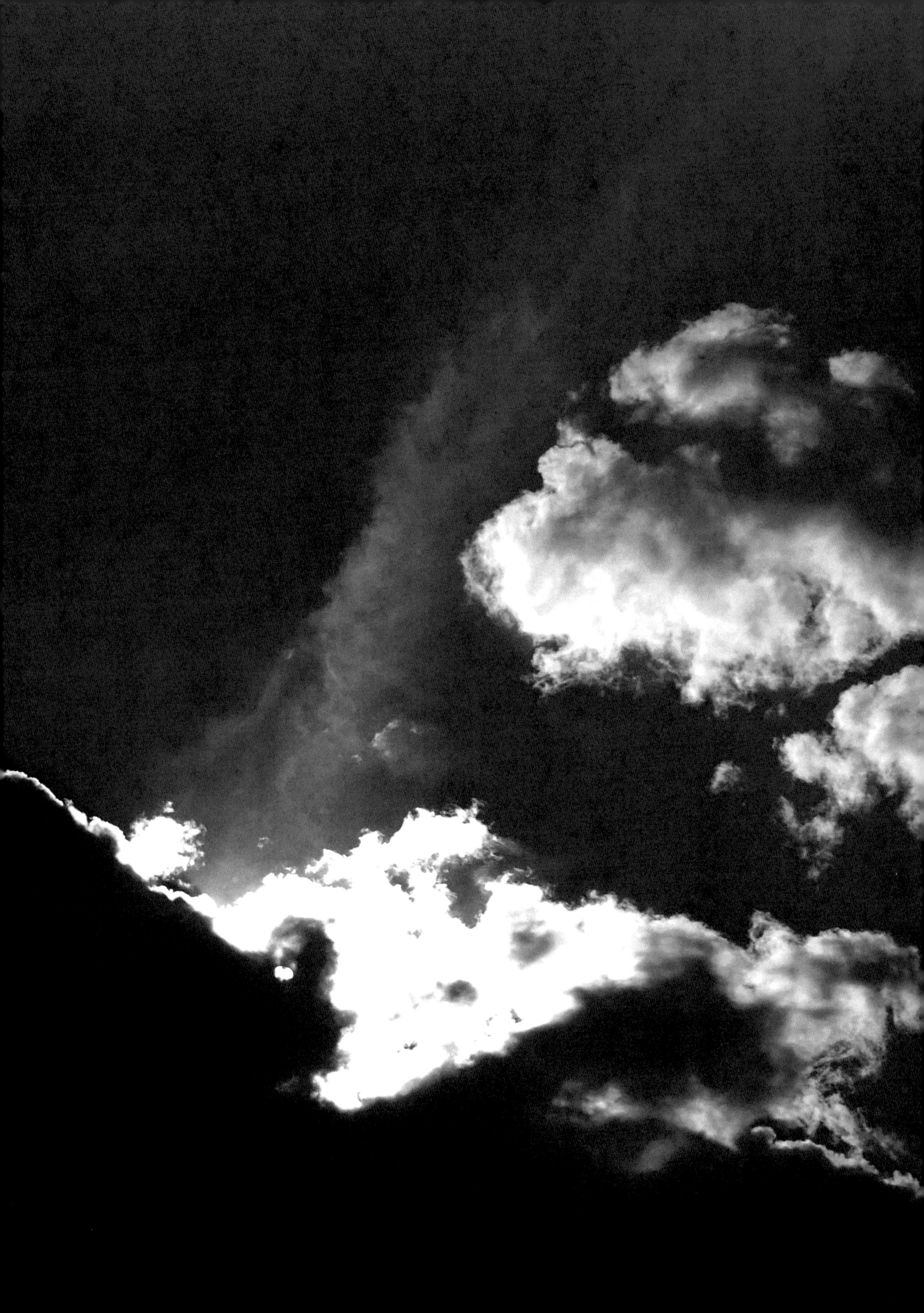

bathroom kind of life. With that being said, once I was living independently, I deeply struggled. I was homeless a few times, I struggled to make a living, and I developed anorexia, some by choice, but also some by circumstance. As I type these words, I understand that I could have gone back home where my grandparents would have ensured that I had a roof, clothing, food, etc, but I was stubborn and on a mission to prove something.

I am not sure what on earth I was trying to prove, but my overall experiences had definitely proven to distort my idea of money at the beginning of my ministry years. I went through a season of having everything I needed as an adolescent, as well as a season of intense lack in my latter years. This led me to this skewed ideology that I can have money, but not too much money because I am a minister of the Gospel. What a messed up view that was! In my finances, I wasn't sure if I was coming or going. It took years of intentional unlearning and relearning to truly have a healthy grasp on my finances. I was recently speaking to a friend about an affiliate marketing gig that I have, where I have successfully sold over $16,000 worth of this company's products. Yes, I have made 10% commission off of said products, but to say there is some untapped potential in my entrepreneurial skills, is an understatement. Part of me stepping into more of my potential is this e-book.

It is okay to believe what God has spoken to you and believe what His Word says! Afterall, our entire lives are predicated on believing what the Bible says concerning salvation and Jesus! God wants to bless you today. Are you ready to receive your blessing?

MY NOTES

MY NOTES

MY NOTES

MY NOTES

MY NOTES

MY NOTES

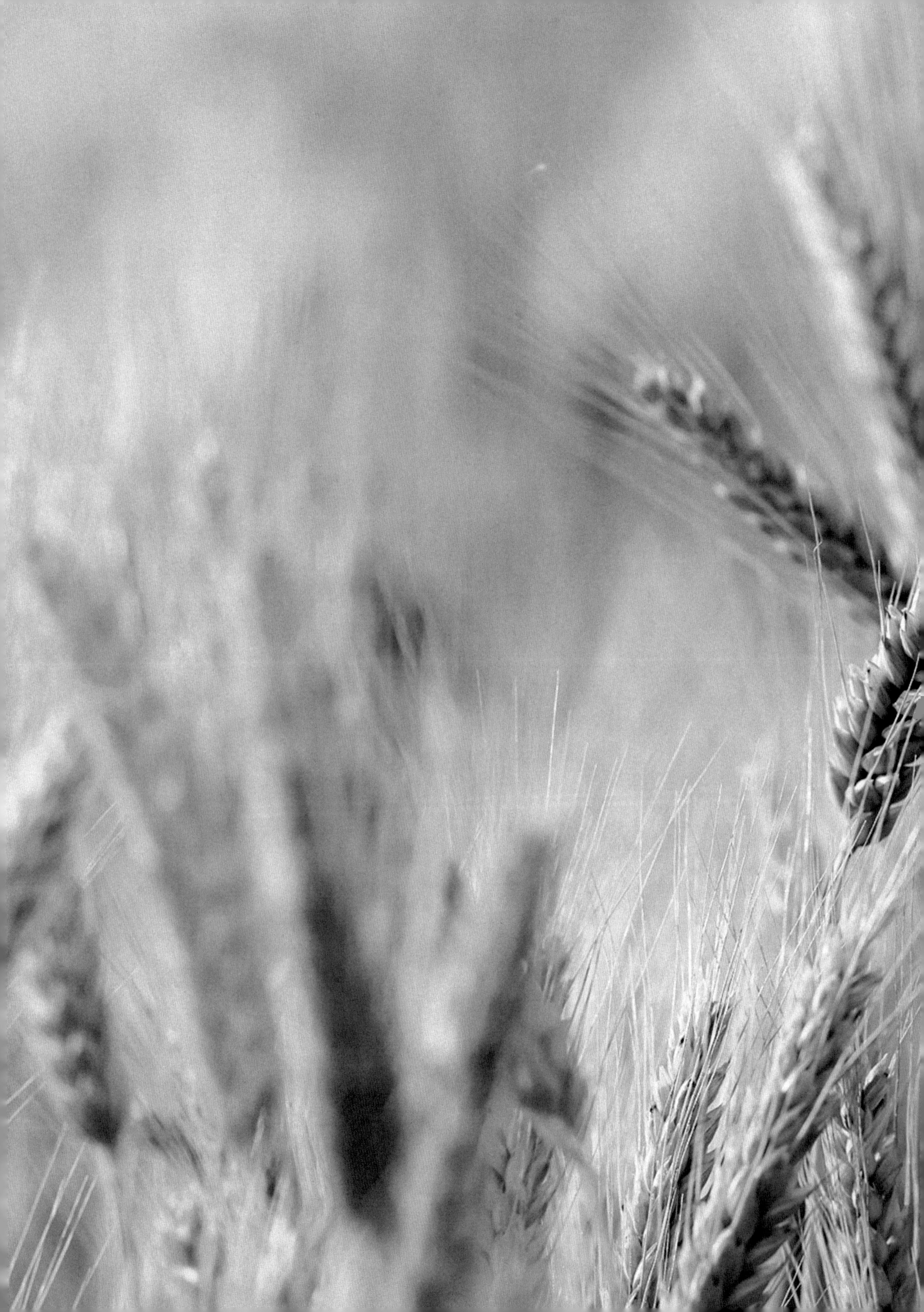

Chapter Four

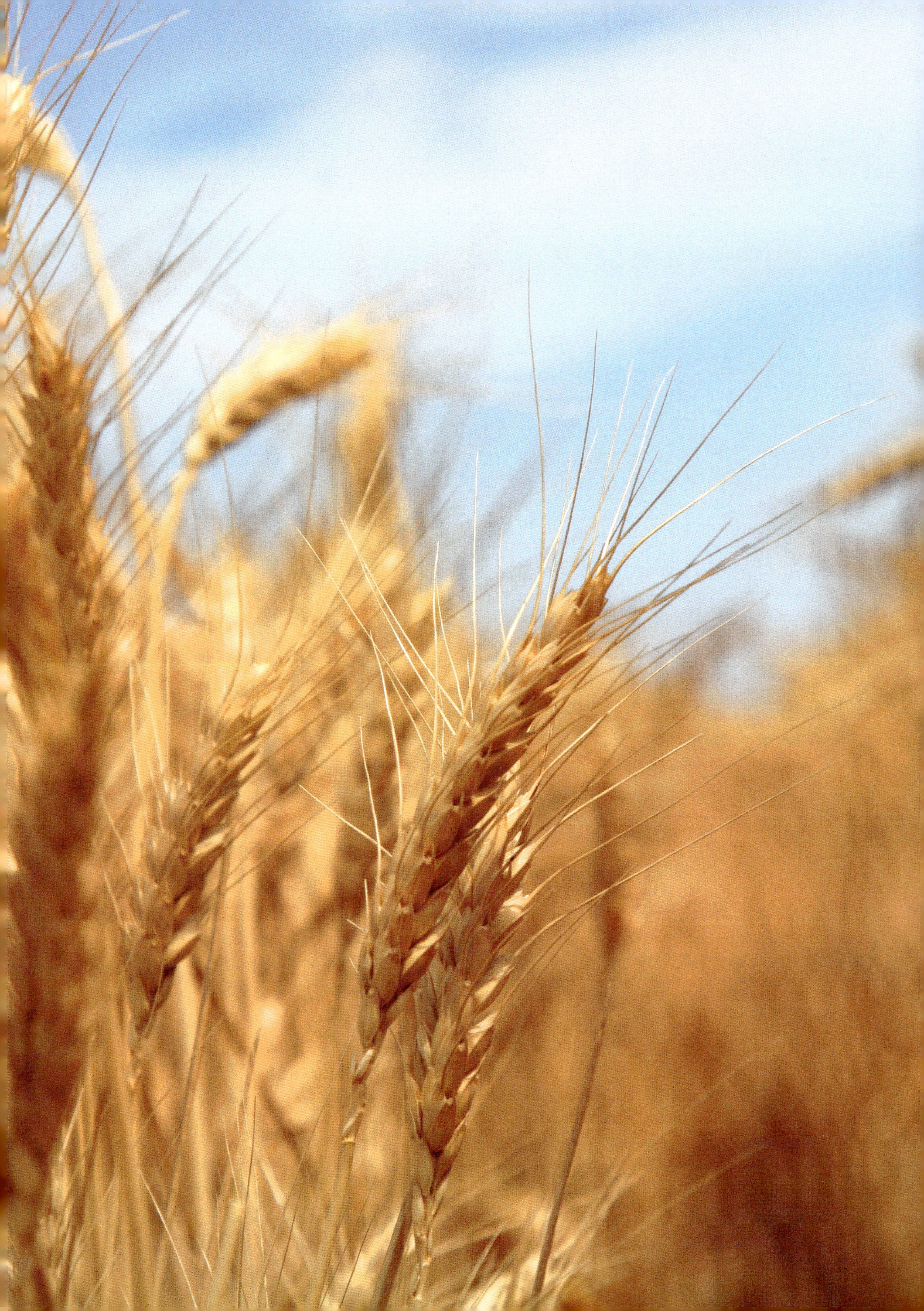

Sow for Harvest

In the Kingdom of God, there are Kingdom principles, and we must obey the principles laid out in scripture to see a full breakthrough in the ways we desire. This revelation has been one I, more recently, truly stepped into, but I have also been faithful to share everything that I have learned with my friends and our church staff. I am even currently preaching on this (at the time of this writing) this Sunday.

A family who serves on our church staff had been waiting for a harvest for many years, but it always seemed like something was holding it up or delaying it. They are business owners and people of radical faith. We had prayed many, many times concerning their finances, and we believed God to breakthrough in this area for them. They remain very faithful in their tithe and in their offering to this day, yet while their daily needs were always met, they hadn't stepped into the abundance that they knew was available to them.

Until now...

I caught this revelation by means of "Financial Success God's Way" by John & Judy O'Leary. I highly recommend finishing this e-book and purchasing that book on Amazon. It has changed everything (and I mean EVERYTHING). I shared this revelation with this faithful family and purchased this financial book for them as seed to plant into good soil. In this chapter, I will give a very brief overview of what I have learned, and if you want an entire book that teaches on what I share here, go grab it! Oh, and I will finish this family's testimony at the end!

Do not tune this part out because you think I am going to say, "pay your tithes and God will bless you." While that is true, that is only part of the actual equation. It is the other part of the equation that takes you from daily needs being met, to an overflow in abundance. Read with intention, and do not read it with a lens as if you know it already. There is a fresh revelation on this for the Church!

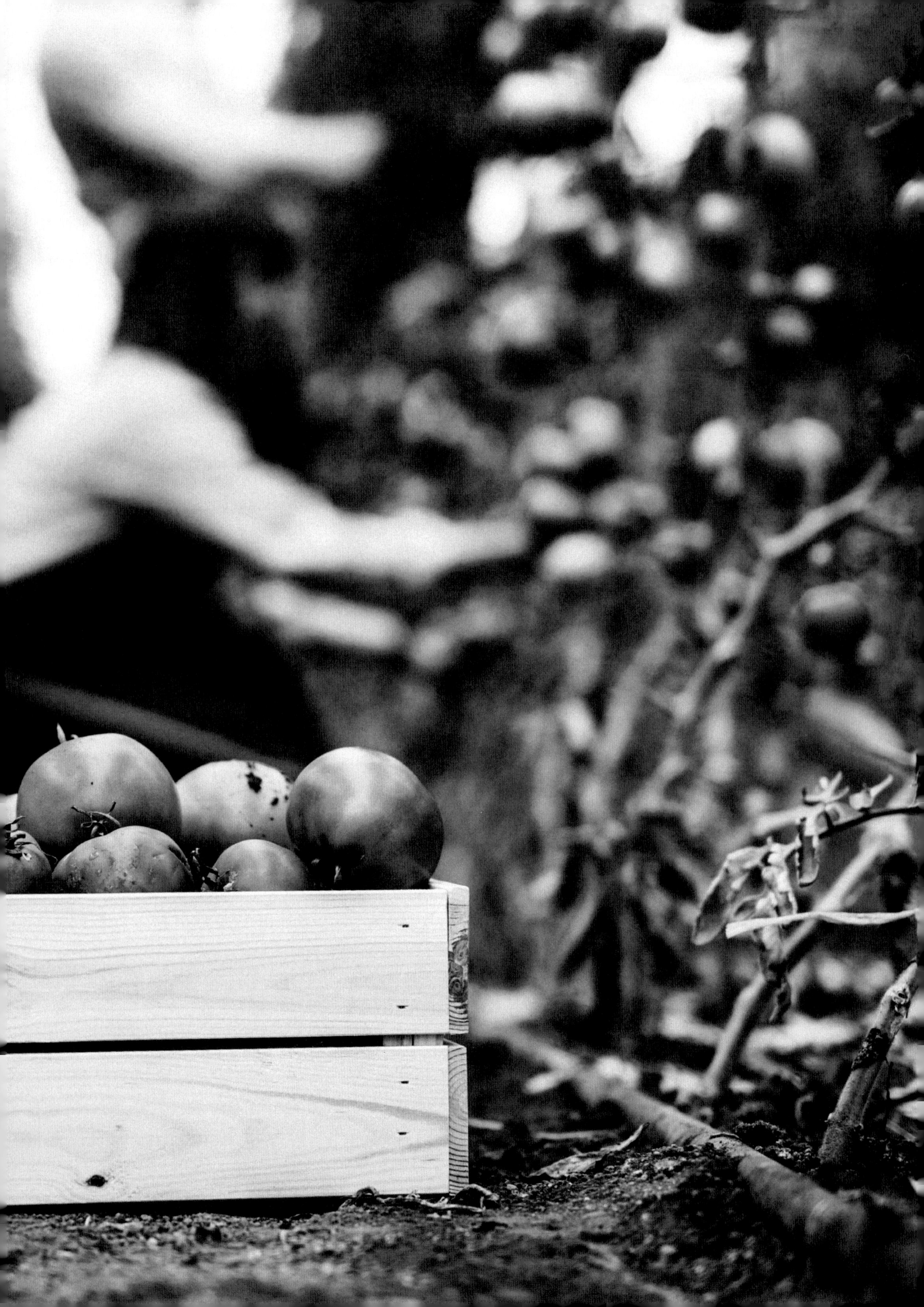

> **"YOU ARE CURSED WITH A CURSE, FOR YOU ARE ROBBING ME, THE WHOLE NATION OF YOU. BRING THE FULL TITHE INTO THE STOREHOUSE, SO THAT THERE MAY BE FOOD IN MY HOUSE. AND THEREBY PUT ME TO THE TEST, SAYS THE LORD OF HOSTS, IF I WILL NOT OPEN THE WINDOWS OF HEAVEN FOR YOU AND POUR DOWN FOR YOU A BLESSING UNTIL THERE IS NO MORE NEED. I WILL REBUKE THE DEVOURER FOR YOU, SO THAT IT WILL NOT DESTROY THE FRUITS OF YOUR SOIL, AND YOUR VINE IN THE FIELD SHALL NOT FAIL TO BEAR, SAYS THE LORD OF HOSTS. THEN ALL NATIONS WILL CALL YOU BLESSED, FOR YOU WILL BE A LAND OF DELIGHT, SAYS THE LORD OF HOSTS."**
> **MALACHI 3:9-12**

The word, tithe, is defined as "honoring God and putting Him first." In John 3:16, we read, "For God so loved the world, He gave his only begotten Son that whoever believes in Him should not perish, but have eternal life." God is generous, and because He is generous, we are also called to generosity.

To give a tithe, it means to give one tenth of an earned income. So, 10% of our income goes to the storehouse; this is where we are spiritually fed, or in simple terms, where we attend services, weekly. The tithe is not just throwing a $20 bill in the offering basket. It is intentionally giving 10% of everything you earn to the church that you attend. The tithe is given first, before anything else is given or spent out of your wages. Romans 11:16 says, "...if the root is holy, so are the branches." You can absolutely give 10% of your wages without it being considered a tithe. The tithe is the first 10%, not the middle or the last.

Consider Cain and Abel. Cain killed Abel because God accepted Abel's sacrifice, but He did not accept Cain's. Why? Abel gave what was first (Genesis 4). You can tithe a full 10% and still not be doing it in accordance with the principle that the tithe is from your first fruits. It takes trust and faith to give the first 10%, and that is what is pleasing to God. His concern is for our heart and our trust in Him. It is not to do with our money. Sunday is like a tithe of our time. We start our week on Sunday; it is the first day of the week, and we begin our week with worshipping Jesus.

Tithing has been a Kingdom principle from the beginning. According to Genesis 14:19-20, Abraham is the first recorded in the scriptures to have given a tenth of everything he possessed.

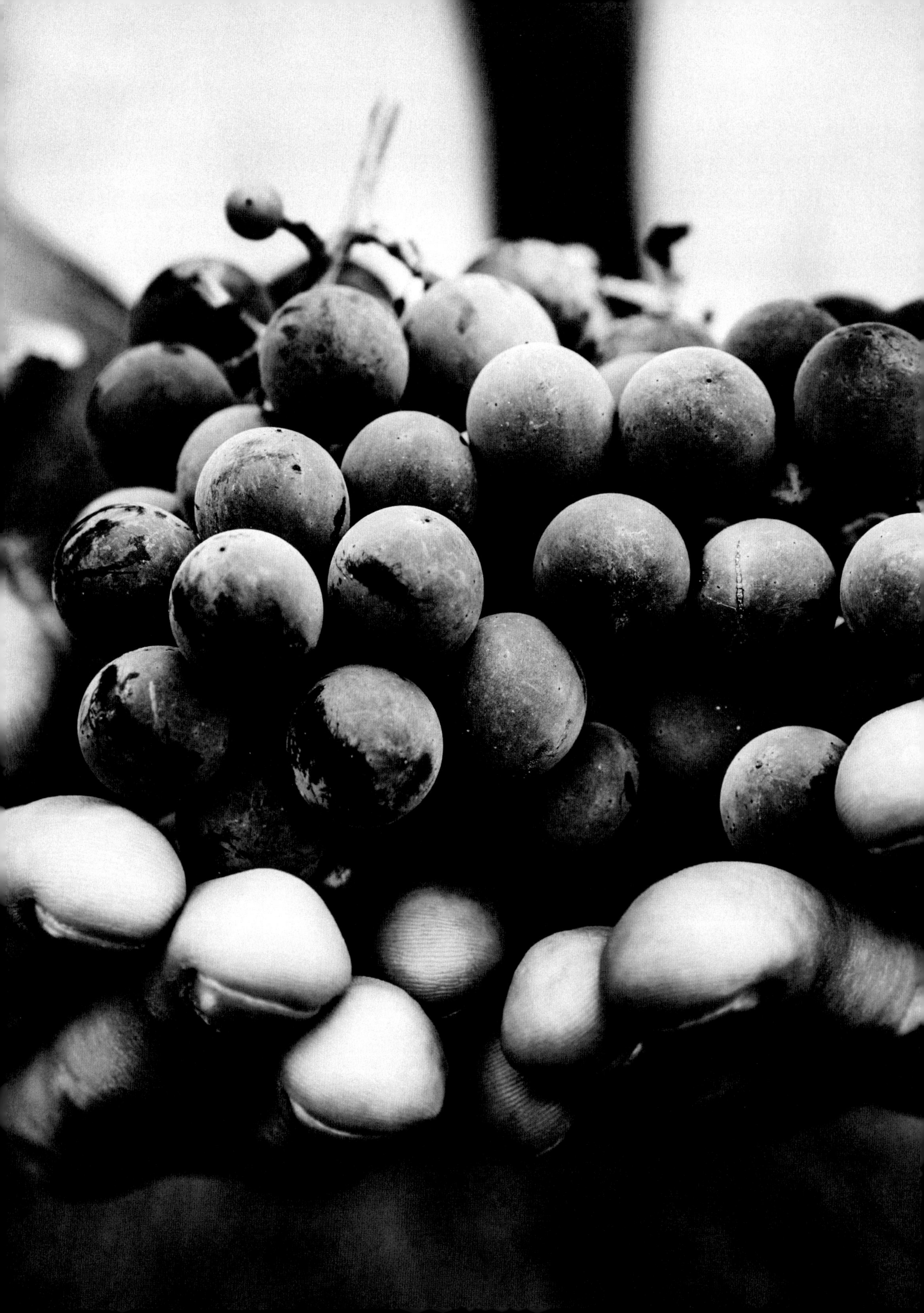

Through this act, the Levites also metaphorically tithed to Melchizedek. Not only did the priest take a tithe from Abraham, but he blessed him. Hebrew's author says, "It is beyond dispute that the inferior is blessed by the superior. (v. 7)" The whole chapter compares the priesthood of Christ to this mysterious Old Testament character, who many scholars believe represented Jesus. So, yes, tithing is for today.

WHAT DOES THE FULL TITHE DO?

1. It removes the curse off of your money. "And now, O priests, this command is for you. If you will not listen, if you will not take it to heart to give honor to my name, says the Lord of hosts, then I will send the curse upon you and I will curse your blessings. Indeed, I have already cursed them, because you do not lay it to heart. Behold, I will rebuke your offspring, and spread dung on your faces, the dung of your offerings, and you shall be taken away with it." Malachi 2:1-31
2. Peter 2:9 says that you are, now, the royal priesthood. Our money is cursed when we do not honor God with our money. God is not after our money, He is after our hearts, friend. If you cannot trust God with your money, you're foolish to think you actually trust Him with your heart.
3. It ensures there is food in the house of God. This means spiritual food to be fed to the congregants, as well as literal food to be provided for those working in the church and those in need within the body.
4. It tests the Lord and evokes Him to move in our lives, gaining trust in our relationship with Him.
5. It releases the blessing of God, and it ensures that we will have no need in our life. All of our daily needs will be met.
6. It rebukes the devourer so that our harvest (from sowing - not from tithing) will be fruitful. (We will get there in a second.)
7. It brings a blessing upon your "nation". Remember that in Biblical times, nations represented families. So, it brings a blessing upon your family, just like withholding it brings a curse on your offspring.

While the tithe ensures that your daily needs are met, first fruits and seeds bring you into an abundant place of overflow. The tithe is like the doorway that we step through, but on the other side of the door is the field in which we sow. The tithe is not where our abundance comes from, but it is where our daily needs and provisions are met. If you tithe, you can expect the curse to be removed, and your daily needs will be met. Yes, your money will be blessed, but the harvest you reap from a tithe is daily provision.

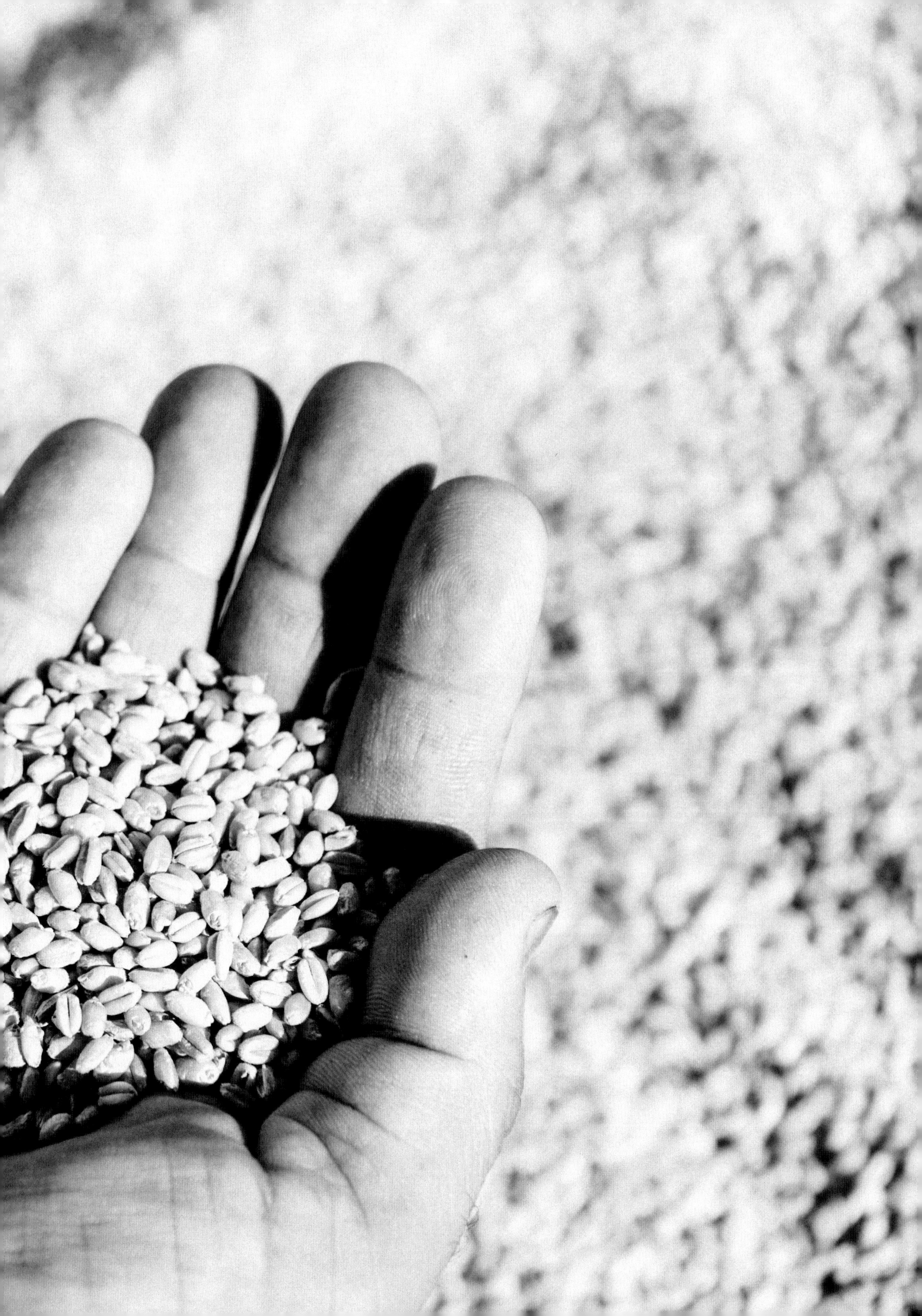

"First fruits", in scripture, referred to the entire first harvest from a field, the first born son, and the first male livestock. These elements were to either be sacrificed for or to be sacrificed. The tithe is our modern day first fruit offering, but our businesses are included in first fruits.

Leviticus 23:10-14 says that "the first fruit is a statute, forever, throughout your generations in all your dwellings." So, it is something that we should never forsake or stop practicing."

Most of us do not own crops or fields, and most of us, being gentiles, do not send our first born sons to the local church to be raised, though, many do practice baby dedication within the church. Most of us do not have livestock, and to further that thought, most churches really don't have much use for a male oxen or rooster. So, how do we observe the first fruits like we are told to do in Leviticus 23:1-14?

"HONOR THE LORD WITH YOUR WEALTH *AND* WITH THE FIRSTFRUITS OF ALL YOUR PRODUCE; *THEN* YOUR BARNS WILL BE FILLED WITH PLENTY, AND YOUR VATS WILL BE BURSTING WITH WINE." PROVERBS 3:9-10

Who gives first fruits? Biblical times were agricultural times. The way the people made a living was through crops, vineyards, livestock, creating linens and other needed items such as tools, baskets, etc. Yes, you could go to work for someone else, but when we see the Lord saying, "honor the Lord with your wealth", we understand that He is speaking of the tithe. Remember, the tithe is honoring the Lord according to Malachi 2. When He is speaking of "the firstfruits of all your produce", He isn't speaking of the produce you would buy at the market. He is speaking to the business owners, telling them that they should give the first fruits of the very thing that brings them wealth. Hence, this is why there is the distinction of honoring the Lord with your wealth, AND honoring Him with your first fruits.

So, if you are a business owner, or have a side hustle, you should give 10% from that income. The first fruits are like the tithe, and they should also be given to the church. Referencing Proverbs 3:9-10, the wealth and first fruits should, both, be given to the "local storehouse" (the Lord). This, likewise, applies to any surplus that you receive, gifts, etc.

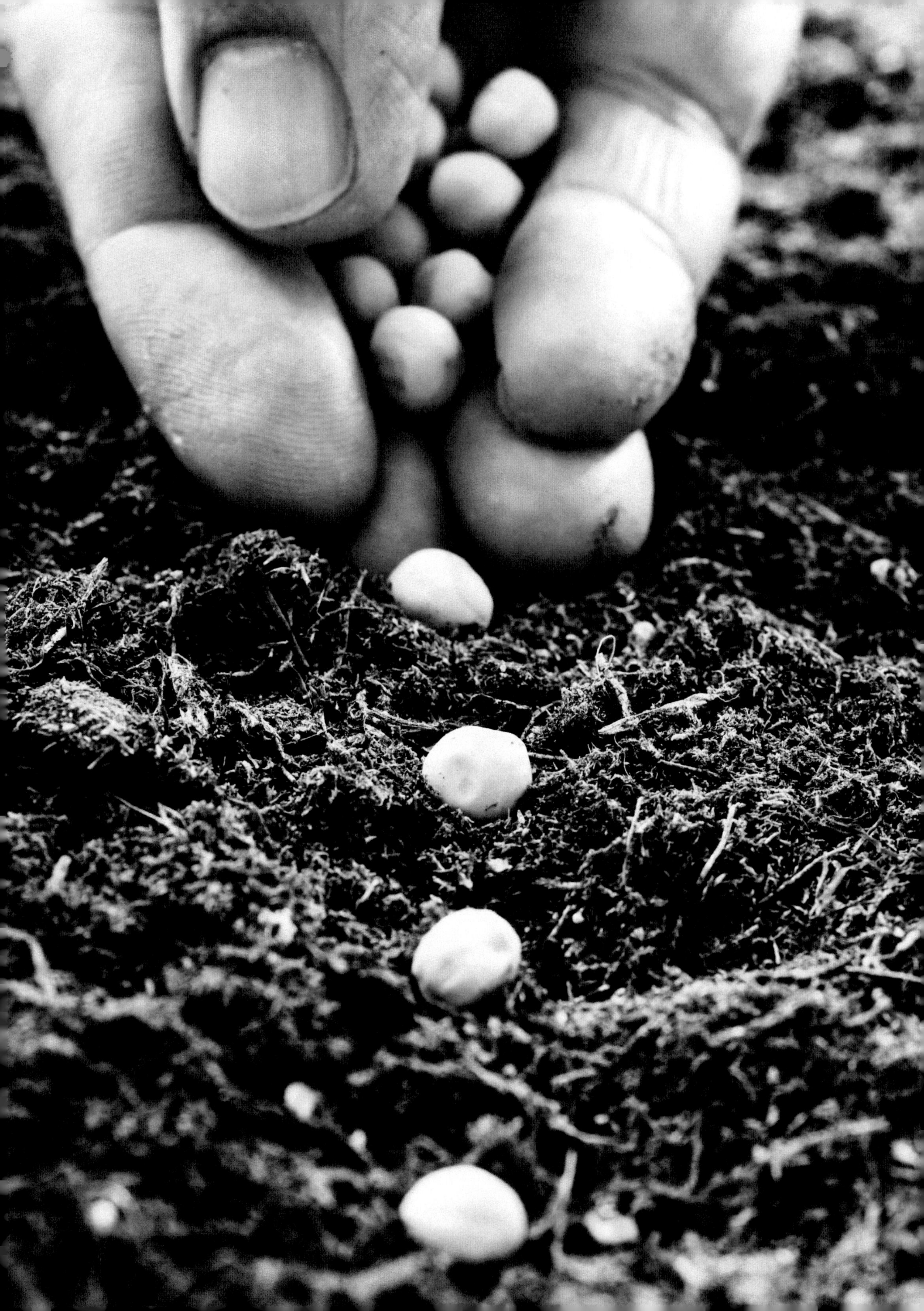

Now, we understand the tithe brings provision for our daily needs, and our first fruits begin to bring us a harvest of provision. Both should be given to the local church. Let's talk about seed/offering; this is the giving that brings rapid acceleration.

> **"THE POINT IS THIS: WHOEVER SOWS SPARINGLY WILL ALSO REAP SPARINGLY, AND WHOEVER SOWS BOUNTIFULLY WILL ALSO REAP BOUNTIFULLY."**
> **2 CORINTHIANS 9:6**

You may have heard it said that faith is the currency of heaven, or honor is the currency of heaven, but I would submit to you that seed is the currency of heaven. You can stand in faith over soil with no seed all day, but if you have failed to put seed into that soil, your faith is without works; therefore, it is dead.

You can prophesy, confess, proclaim, and decree all day, but if you have no seed in the ground, you have nothing that can yield a harvest. Many of us are trying to reap a harvest from our tithe, but the harvest from our tithe is that our NEEDS are met, and our harvest FROM OUR SEED is protected. The tithe is the door we walk through to receive abundance, but on the other side of the door is the field where we plant the seeds!

> **"LISTEN TO ME; LISTEN, AND PAY CLOSE ATTENTION. DOES A FARMER ALWAYS PLOW AND NEVER SOW? IS HE FOREVER CULTIVATING THE SOIL AND NEVER PLANTING SEED?"**
> **ISAIAH 28:23-24**

Everything comes from a seed; even weeds come from seeds! You can only reap from what you have sown. No matter what you are sowing, you are reaping. It is His law. This includes your time, emotions, thoughts, etc. For the sake of today, we are speaking on finances, but this law is universal and touches all areas of life. Galatians 6:7 says, "Do not be deceived, God is not mocked; for whatever a man sows, that he will also reap."

Genesis 1:11 says, "...the seeds will produce the kinds of plants and trees from which they came," so what you plant is what will grow.

> **"...AS LONG AS THE EARTH REMAINS, THE LAW OF SEEDTIME AND HARVEST WILL NEVER CEASE." GENESIS 8:22**

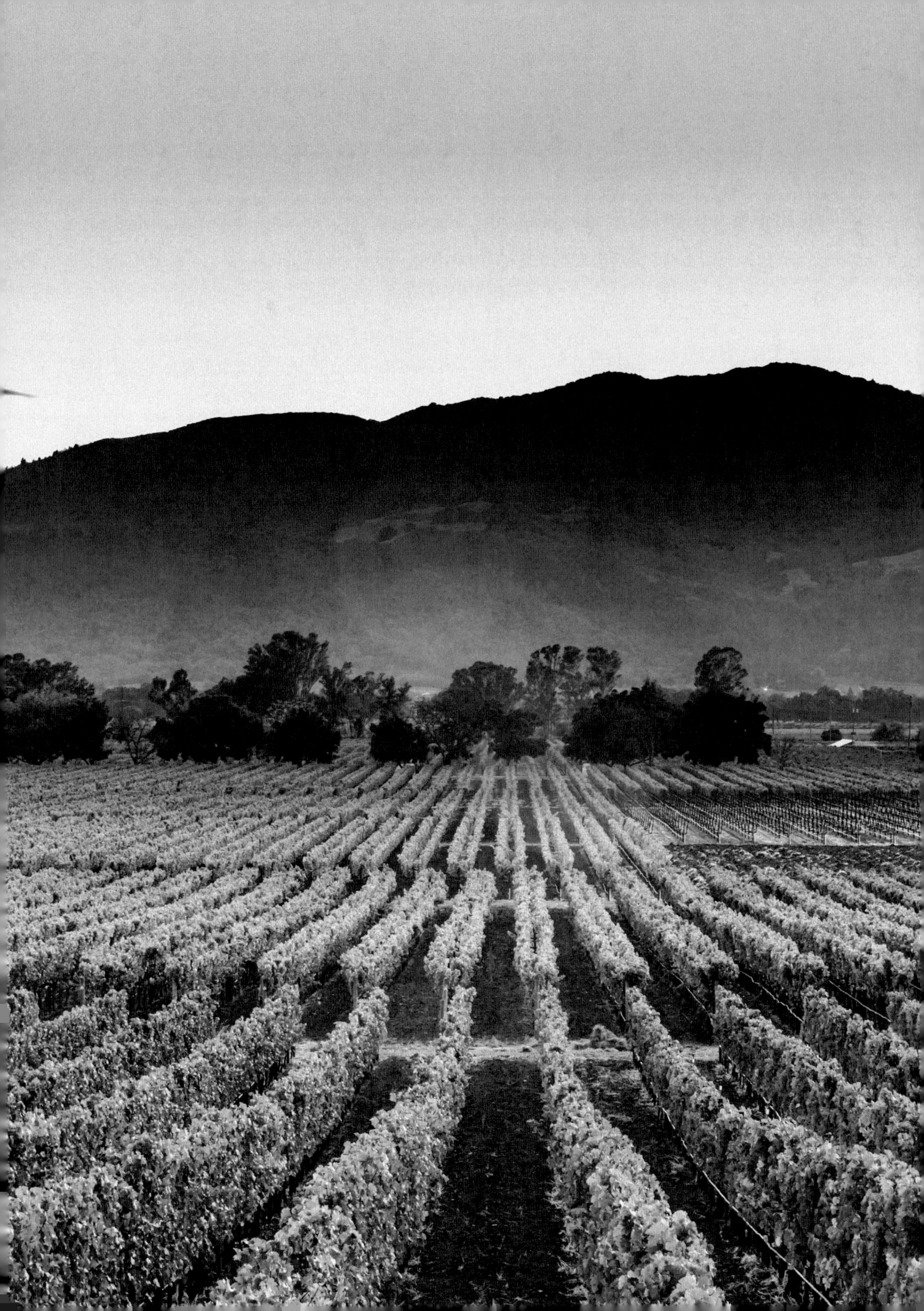

1. A seed can only produce itself. If I plant a cucumber seed, I do not expect a pumpkin to grow. This means the seed you sow is what will grow.
2. You will reap if you sow. It is His law.
3. His law isn't going to change. Ever.

God loves us, He hears our faith-filled confessions, and He wants to see us step into increase, but we must understand His Word and law. Psalms 138:2 says, "For you have magnified Your word above all Your name."

If God gave you a harvest without seed, He would be violating His own Word, and He has made His Word even above His own name. God has so chosen to obey His own laws, we KNOW we can trust Him. Financial deliverance is not just deliverance from a poverty spirit or a religious mindset (while demonic spirits and teaching can be at play), but financial deliverance comes from and is sustained through THE SEED.

There is a difference between simply sowing seed and being a sower. We want to become sowers. Sowers look for good fertile soil where their seed can be sown. Sowers understand that when they sow, they reap. We do not give our tithe to get, but a promise from our seed is that we will reap what we sow. Period. A great example of a purposeful sower in scripture is the Queen of Sheba in 1 Kings 10:1-13

In the first verse, the queen of Sheba heard of Solomon's fame, which brought honor to the name of the Lord, so she came to test him with hard questions. She heard the soil was good, but she was ready to sow big. She wanted to make sure the soil was truly good, so she went to test him. Never sow into untested soil. Let me say that again. NEVER sow into UNTESTED soil. We must walk in our financial anointing with wisdom, and we must be good stewards of what God has given us.

"SHE ARRIVED AT JERUSALEM WITH A LARGE GROUP OF ATTENDANTS AND A GREAT CARAVAN OF CAMELS LOADED WITH SPICES, LARGE QUANTITIES OF GOLD, AND PRECIOUS JEWELS. WHEN SHE MET WITH SOLOMON, SHE TALKED WITH HIM ABOUT EVERYTHING SHE HAD ON HER MIND. SOLOMON HAD ANSWERS FOR ALL HER QUESTIONS; NOTHING WAS TOO HARD FOR THE KING TO EXPLAIN TO HER. WHEN THE QUEEN OF SHEBA REALIZED HOW VERY WISE SOLOMON WAS, AND WHEN SHE SAW THE PALACE HE HAD BUILT, SHE WAS OVERWHELMED. SHE WAS ALSO AMAZED AT THE FOOD ON HIS TABLES, THE ORGANIZATION OF HIS OFFICIALS AND THEIR SPLENDID CLOTHING, THE CUP-BEARERS, AND THE BURNT OFFERINGS SOLOMON MADE AT THE TEMPLE OF

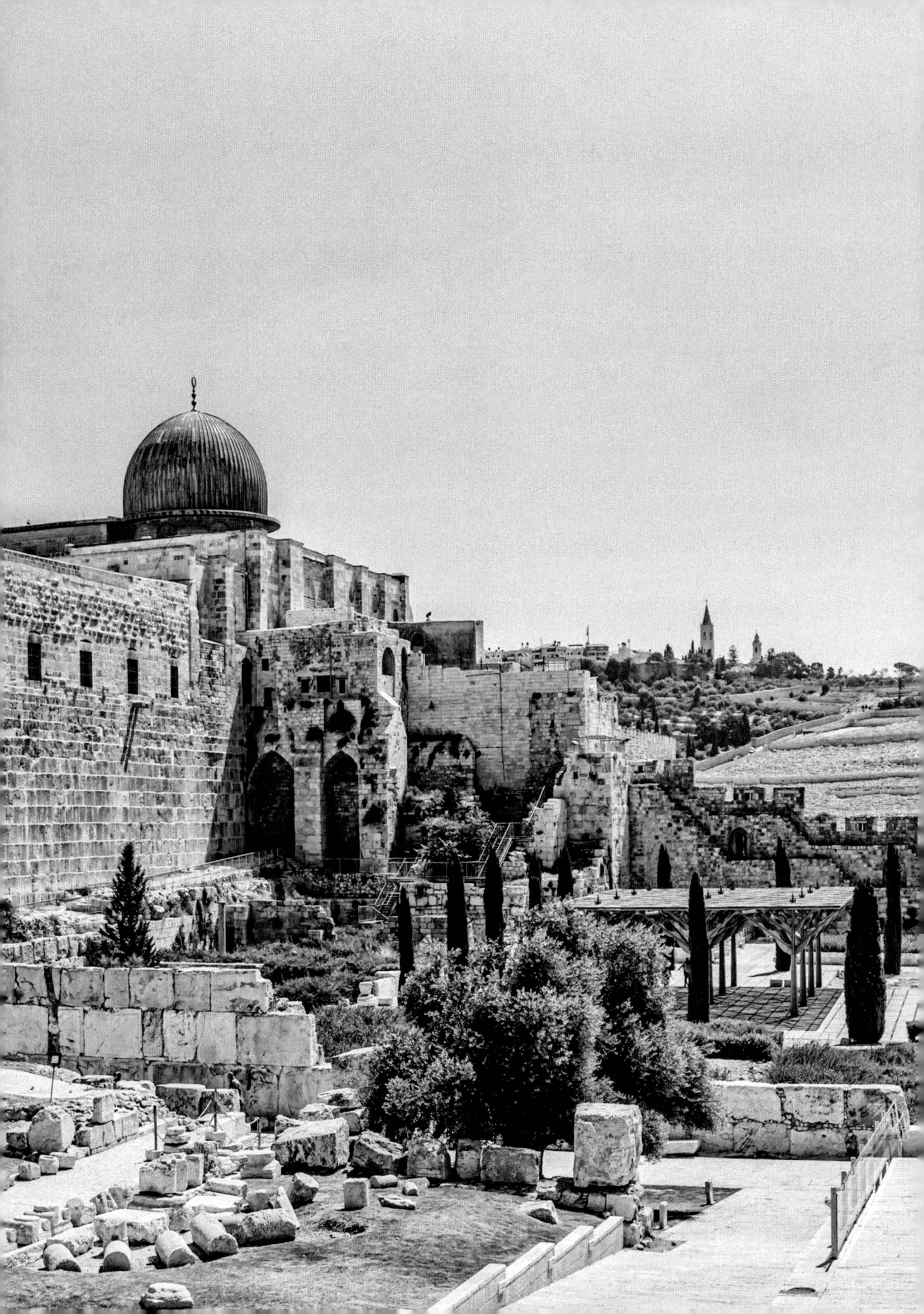

THE LORD. SHE EXCLAIMED TO THE KING, "EVERYTHING I HEARD IN MY COUNTRY ABOUT YOUR ACHIEVEMENTS AND WISDOM IS TRUE! I DIDN'T BELIEVE WHAT WAS SAID UNTIL I ARRIVED HERE AND SAW IT WITH MY OWN EYES. IN FACT, I HAD NOT HEARD THE HALF OF IT! YOUR WISDOM AND PROSPERITY ARE FAR BEYOND WHAT I WAS TOLD. HOW HAPPY YOUR PEOPLE MUST BE! WHAT A PRIVILEGE FOR YOUR OFFICIALS TO STAND HERE DAY AFTER DAY, LISTENING TO YOUR WISDOM! PRAISE THE LORD YOUR GOD, WHO DELIGHTS IN YOU AND HAS PLACED YOU ON THE THRONE OF ISRAEL. BECAUSE OF THE LORD'S ETERNAL LOVE FOR ISRAEL, HE HAS MADE YOU KING SO YOU CAN RULE WITH JUSTICE AND RIGHTEOUSNESS." 1 KINGS 10:2-9

Let's make one thing very clear: God got the glory for Solomon's extravagant wealth, and He will get the glory for your wealth too. People who tell you that God only wants your bare needs to be met, simply haven't understood the principles of the Kingdom. Some believe that taking a vow of poverty is noble, spiritual, and even Godly, but if you barely have enough to meet your own needs, how will you help meet the needs of others? How will you leave an inheritance for your children?

Wealth is not demonic. Money, itself, does not change someone. It simply brings to light who they already were and/or are. If you were generous before, you'll be generous after. If you were greedy before, you'll be greedy after. Money is just a tool, and it has no power to change a person; it just has the power to put on display what was already inside of you.

Let's finish with Queen of Sheba & Solomon:

"THEN SHE GAVE THE KING A GIFT OF 9,000 POUNDS[D] OF GOLD, GREAT QUANTITIES OF SPICES, AND PRECIOUS JEWELS. NEVER AGAIN WERE SO MANY SPICES BROUGHT IN AS THOSE THE QUEEN OF SHEBA GAVE TO KING SOLOMON. (IN ADDITION, HIRAM'S SHIPS BROUGHT GOLD FROM OPHIR, AND THEY ALSO BROUGHT RICH CARGOES OF RED SANDALWOOD[E] AND PRECIOUS JEWELS. THE KING USED THE SANDALWOOD TO MAKE RAILINGS FOR THE TEMPLE OF THE LORD AND THE ROYAL PALACE, AND TO CONSTRUCT LYRES AND HARPS FOR THE MUSICIANS. NEVER BEFORE OR SINCE HAS THERE BEEN SUCH A SUPPLY OF SANDALWOOD.) KING SOLOMON GAVE THE QUEEN OF SHEBA WHATEVER SHE ASKED FOR, BESIDES ALL THE CUSTOMARY GIFTS HE HAD SO GENEROUSLY GIVEN. THEN SHE AND ALL HER ATTENDANTS RETURNED TO THEIR OWN LAND."
1 KINGS 10:10-13

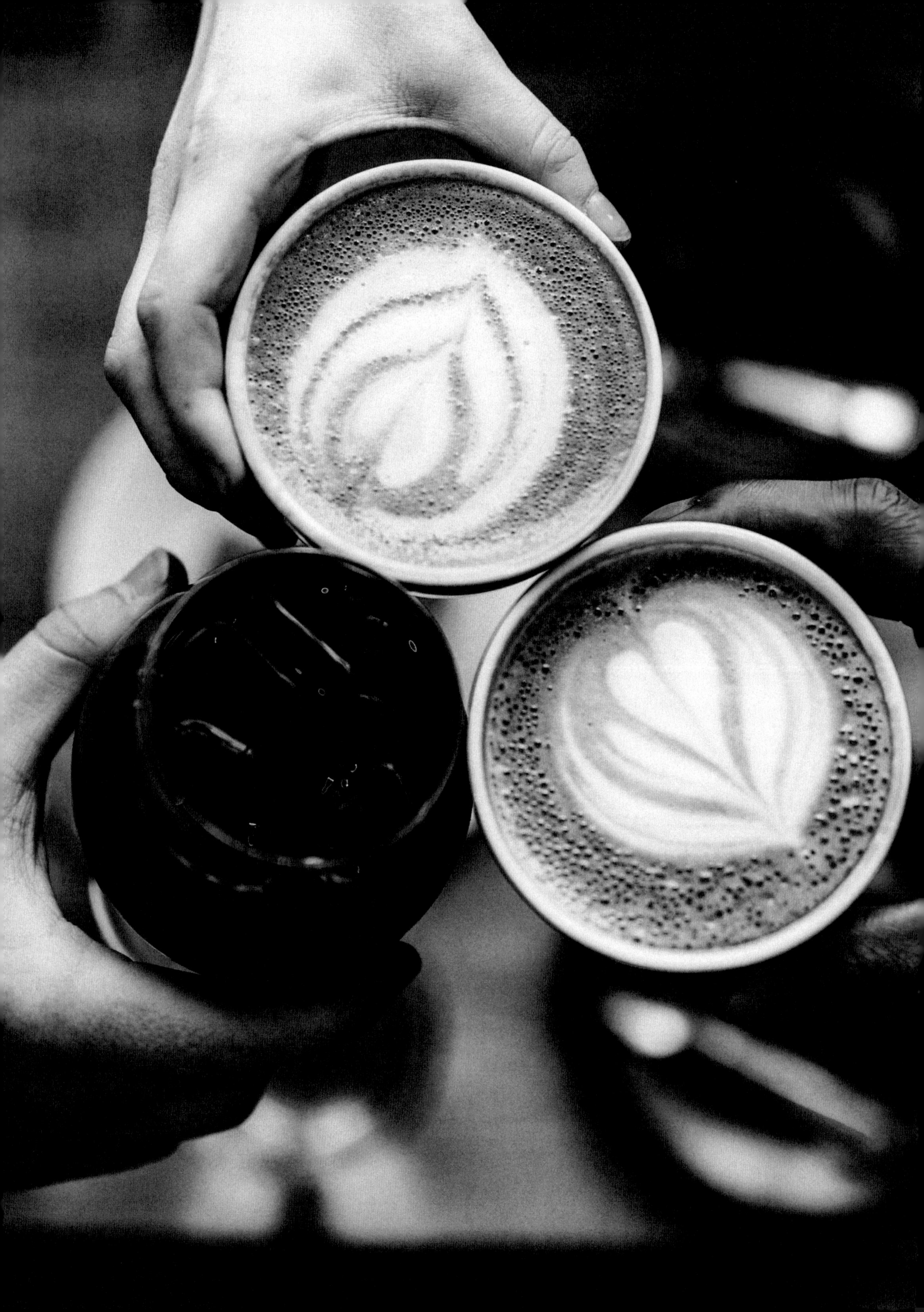

Wow! Did Solomon need anything from the queen? No. Did her giving meet a NEED in the Kingdom? No. She still sowed into the harvest, though, because she wanted to receive. Solomon was a miracle soil for her. Paul understood this when he told the Philippians in Phillippians 4:17, "...not that I desire your gifts; what I desire is that more be credited to your account."

Everyone has something to sow. Some seed is for sowing, and some seed is for eating. Genesis 1:29 says, "Then God said, 'Look, I have given you every seed-bearing plant throughout the earth AND all the fruit trees for your food.'" And 2 Corinthians 9:10 says, "Now he who supplies seed to the sower AND bread for food will also supply and increase your store of seed and will enlarge the harvest of your righteousness." God WILL give you seed. If you feel that you are maxed out at your tithe, but you desire to sow, and you are asking yourself how you can sow without having the seed to do so, ask God for seed. He gives seed to the sower!

Don't eat the seed! If you eat it, that is all it will ever be. You will have consumed your future. The seed can only produce a harvest once it has been released. The seed, by itself, does not have the power to produce. It must be put in the ground. The purpose of the seed is not to bless the soil, but to bring a harvest to the sower. That is why it is truly more blessed to give, than it is to receive (Acts 20:35). Jesus is the incorruptible seed, and He is also the Lord of the harvest. His Spirit is alive within us! Sowing and reaping is engrafted into our DNA.

The soil represents the "what" or "who" in which we are sowing our seed. The soil we sow into is just as crucial as the seed we sow. The soil is what nourishes the seed, so if there are not healthy properties in the soil, the harvest will reflect it. The soil can only yield what it holds. It is our job, as a sower, to find the good soil that will produce a harvest. You can sow into a church, a ministry, a person, a business, an idea, etc. You can sow seed anywhere because it is your seed to direct. Mark 4 and Matthew 13 tell us that seed can and will be wasted if we don't sow into the right soil.

"LISTEN! BEHOLD, A SOWER WENT OUT TO SOW. AND AS HE SOWED, SOME SEED FELL ALONG THE PATH, AND THE BIRDS CAME AND DEVOURED IT. OTHER SEED FELL ON ROCKY GROUND, WHERE IT DID NOT HAVE MUCH SOIL, AND IMMEDIATELY IT SPRANG UP, SINCE IT HAD NO DEPTH OF SOIL. AND WHEN THE SUN ROSE, IT WAS SCORCHED, AND SINCE IT HAD NO ROOT, IT WITHERED AWAY. OTHER SEED FELL

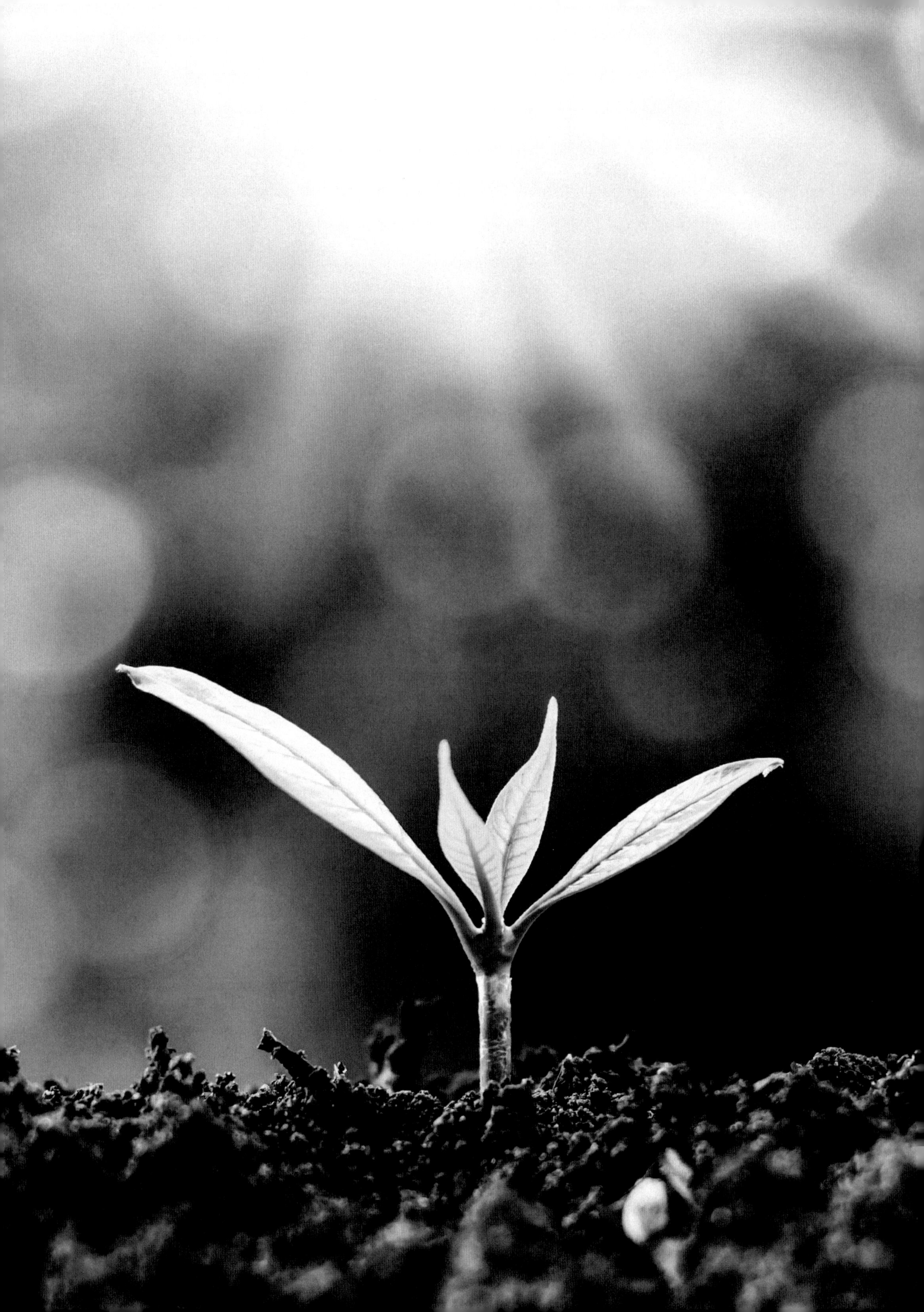

among thorns, and the thorns grew up and choked it, and it yielded no grain. And other seeds fell into good soil and produced grain, growing up and increasing and yielding thirtyfold and sixtyfold and a hundredfold." And he said, "He who has ears to hear, let him hear.'" Mark 4:3-9**

The soil is crucial. You can take a very potent and able seed and put it in the wrong soil, causing you to reap no harvest. Likewise, understand that 100, 60, and 30-fold yield was dependent upon the potential in the seed sown. Each seed has potential.

"And he said to them, "Do you not understand this parable? How then will you understand all the parables?'" Mark 4:13

Jesus said if we don't understand this principle, we don't understand any of the other parables. Why? It is because the Kingdom of God operates on the law of reaping and sowing.

When you sow, the harvest is yours, and that is a hard fact. Remember that because of the tithe, the Lord will rebuke the devourer for you, so that it will not destroy the fruits of your soil, and your vine in the field shall not fail to bear. The moment you sow, it is rightfully yours. Your seed reaches into your future, blesses it, and you walk right into the promise. When God asks you to sow a seed, rejoice! He has your harvest in mind! God will never be in debt to a sower. Galatians 6:9 says, "Let us not become weary in doing good, for at the proper time we will reap a harvest if we do not give up."

There is something very special about giving, and it moves God because He is THE Giver. We are living out the mission of being Christ-like when we are being givers.

**"Give to the Lord the glory he deserves! Bring your offering and come into his presence. Worship the Lord in all his holy splendor."
1 Chronicles 16:29**

You can sing and worship until you are blue in the face, and while it will move the heart of God, it will not move His hand because He obeys His law. Giving is what moves the hand of God into action in your life. Luke 6:38 says, "Give and it will be given to you; good measure, pressed down, shaken together, and running over,

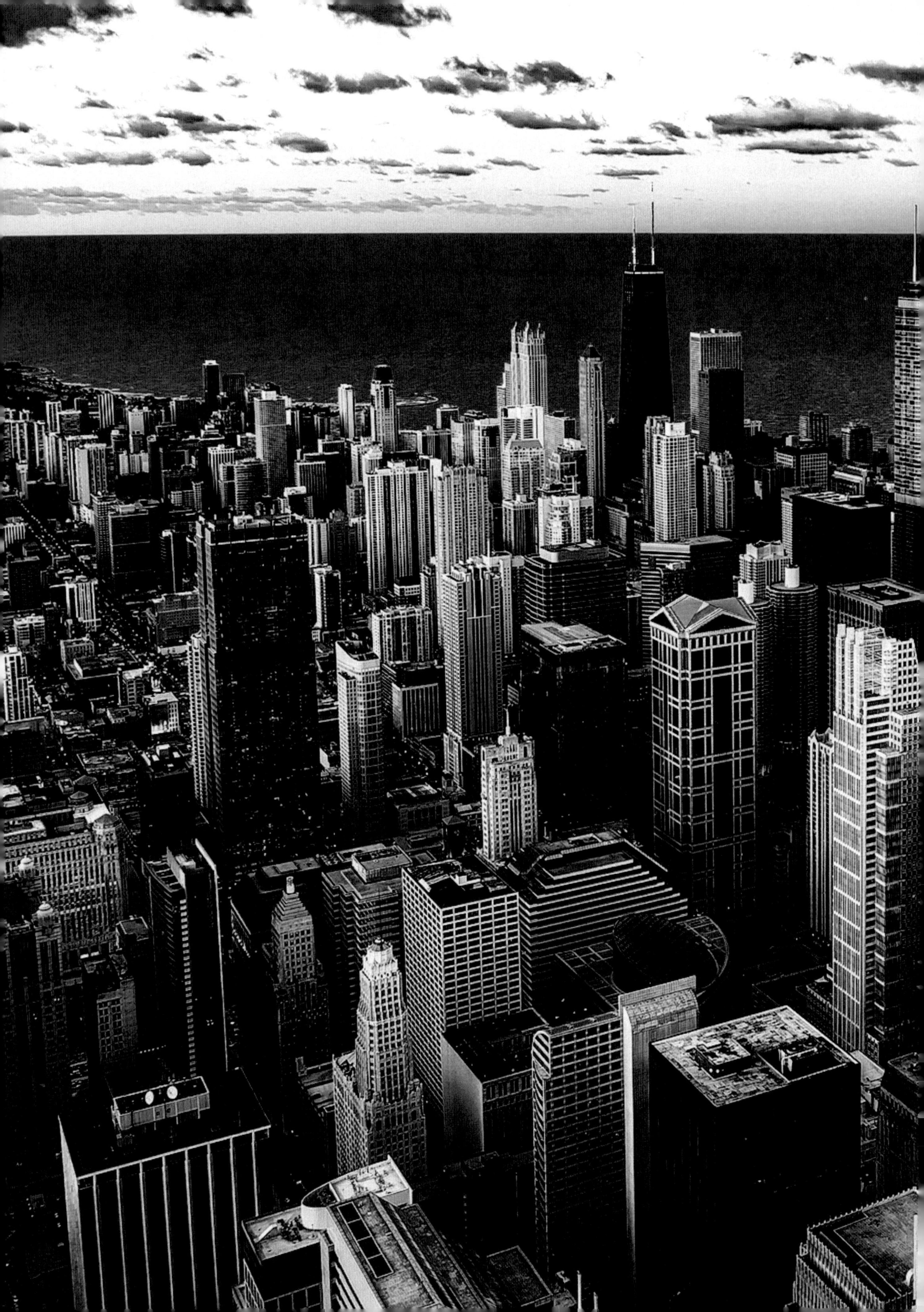

shall men give into your bosom." The measure in which we give determines how much we receive, and the soil in which we sow determines what we receive in return. When we give our best, we get God's best. God's best is unmatched!

Likewise, remember that when you begin to reap a harvest, it can also come as a witty invention like we talked about earlier. Discern your harvest! Ask God to help you recognize when your harvest comes! Your harvest might come as an action step that you need to take, so listen to those little nudges and be bold to step into what God is calling you to so that you can receive your full harvest.

"HE WHO HAS PITY ON THE POOR LENDS TO THE LORD, AND HE WILL PAY BACK WHAT HE HAS GIVEN." PROVERBS 19:17

Alms, giving to the poor, and meeting needs is not multiplied back to you. God gives back what you give. You could think of this type of investment as a dollar-for-dollar return. Jesus expects us to give to the poor as a part of our Christian duty. We do not do this to receive abundance from such a type of giving.

There is, however, one other thing that you will receive from giving to the poor, aside from the initial payback of what was given, and that is health. Isaiah 58:7-8 tells us that when we give to the poor and help meet their needs, the healing of the Lord will spring up, suddenly. If you need healing in your body, you need to start meeting the NEEDS of the poor. This is not seed, offering, or tithe. This is meeting a real need.

In the area of alms:
1. We don't give our best to alms because our best is reserved for God and our seed. That is, straight up, Bible. We are to allow the poor to glean from the edges of the field, as the scripture says. Paul writes in 2 Corinthians 8:13-14, "Of course, I don't mean your giving should make life easy for others and hard for yourselves. I only mean that there should be some equality. your abundance at the present time should supply their need, so that their abundance may supply your need, that there may be fairness."

Notice, scripture says out of your abundance, not out of your lack or daily wages. How do we receive abundance to have enough to give in addition? Seed. This is why we need to renew our mind in the area of wealth and business as Christians. We have to have enough to give.

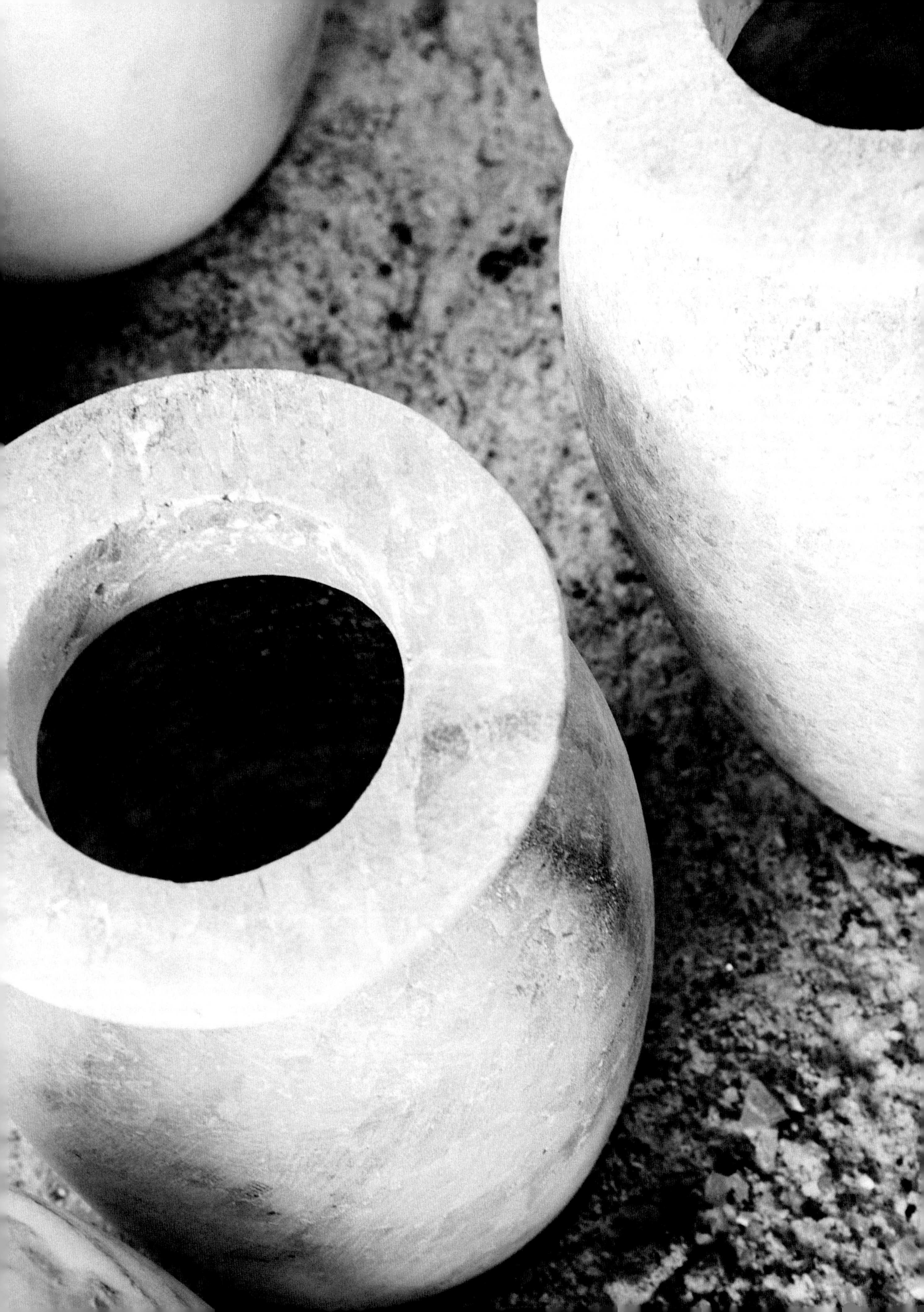

2. The Bible says to leave the edges of your fields for the poor to glean; it does not say pick it, and give it to them. Giving in this way makes us feel good, but it strips the poor of their dignity, which is also why the Bible says to give to the poor in secret so that their dignity will be protected.

When we give benevolently as a church, there are many cases in which not even the entire staff knows that we are giving. We purposefully allocate funds for that, that way, dignity is honored and protected.

3. Don't expect or ask for a harvest. Alms are not seeds; they are a loan to the Lord that He repays. If you don't want to reap poverty, then do not proclaim your giving to the poor as a seed, and do not ask for a harvest in return. Remember that the soil you sow into determines the harvest you will reap. The soil will produce what it holds, and the poor give through poverty.

I am not saying to not give to the poor! That is part of our christian duty. I am saying that we need to be aware of how to give to the poor in the Biblical context. It is very important that we are able to identify these things for our full understanding of all scripture concerning giving.

Remember that a religious and betraying spirit and mindset says that seed should be given to the poor. Consider Judas, for example:

"NOW, WHEN JESUS WAS AT BETHANY IN THE HOUSE OF SIMON THE LEPER, A WOMAN CAME UP TO HIM WITH AN ALABASTER FLASK OF VERY EXPENSIVE OINTMENT, AND SHE POURED IT ON HIS HEAD AS HE RECLINED AT TABLE. AND WHEN THE DISCIPLES SAW IT, THEY WERE INDIGNANT, SAYING, "WHY THIS WASTE? FOR THIS COULD HAVE BEEN SOLD FOR A LARGE SUM AND GIVEN TO THE POOR." BUT JESUS, AWARE OF THIS, SAID TO THEM, "WHY DO YOU TROUBLE THE WOMAN? FOR SHE HAS DONE A BEAUTIFUL THING TO ME. FOR YOU ALWAYS HAVE THE POOR WITH YOU, BUT YOU WILL NOT ALWAYS HAVE ME. IN POURING THIS OINTMENT ON MY BODY, SHE HAS DONE IT TO PREPARE ME FOR BURIAL. TRULY, I SAY TO YOU, WHEREVER THIS GOSPEL IS PROCLAIMED IN THE WHOLE WORLD, WHAT SHE HAS DONE WILL ALSO BE TOLD IN MEMORY OF HER." THEN ONE OF THE TWELVE, WHOSE NAME WAS JUDAS ISCARIOT, WENT TO THE CHIEF PRIESTS AND SAID, "WHAT WILL YOU GIVE ME IF I DELIVER HIM OVER TO YOU?" AND THEY PAID HIM THIRTY PIECES OF SILVER. AND FROM THAT MOMENT HE SOUGHT AN OPPORTUNITY TO BETRAY HIM." MATTHEW 26: 6-16

The key word there for me is, "then". THEN, Judas decided he was going to hand over Jesus in betrayal. Abundance and wealth have always made the religious mad. I am not 100% sure why, but I do know that is a truth that we see all throughout the Bible. Do not let this deter you from pressing into the more of God that He has for you.

He has given you a creative ability to think, and He desires to give you witty ideas! It is Biblical to believe that He will bless you, and when you are ready to step in, I urge you to start giving. Test Him at His Word! I truly believe that these principles have the potential to change anyone's life, if they allow it. Oh! About that family that just caught the revelation of sowing and reaping, within days of beginning to sow they began to receive checks and unexpected blessings. The first check was for $1,000, the second one was for $2,000 and the blessings continue to blow all of our minds.

Let's pray.

Father,
Thank You for the creative genius that You have placed on the inside of me. Thank You for the ability you have given me to think and find solutions to today's problems. I ask that You give me witty ideas and inventions. I submit my mind to You, and I ask that You would think through me, Lord. I pray that you would cause me to be attentive to know when You are thinking and speaking to and through me, so I can move forward with the ideas you are giving me. Father, if I am bound by a spirit of religion or poverty, I pray that you would liberate me now in the mighty name of Jesus. Your Word says that a good man leaves an inheritance for his children and grandchildren, so Lord, I pray that I have the ideas and resources to do that for my family. I pray that You would show me how, and illuminate the path You have for me.

I ask that You help me to be faithful in my tithe and first fruits, that You would bless my pastors and my church, Lord. Father, please give me seed and show me every bit of good ground, so that I can sow where accordingly. Send seed in many forms, and please cause me to not only realize when You have sent the seed, but also where You desire for it to be sown. Likewise, I ask that You help me recognize the harvest when it comes. I thank You for the harvest, even now, Father. You are so good, so loving, and so merciful. Thank You for this revelation, that I may continue to walk in it. In Jesus name, amen.

MY NOTES

MY NOTES

MY NOTES

MY NOTES

MY NOTES

MY NOTES

MY NOTES

MY NOTES

MY NOTES

MY NOTES

MY NOTES

MY NOTES

MY NOTES

MY NOTES

MY NOTES

MY NOTES

MY NOTES

MY NOTES

MY NOTES

MY NOTES

MY NOTES

MY NOTES

MY NOTES

MY NOTES

MY NOTES

MY NOTES

MY NOTES

MY NOTES

MY NOTES

MY NOTES

JOSEPH

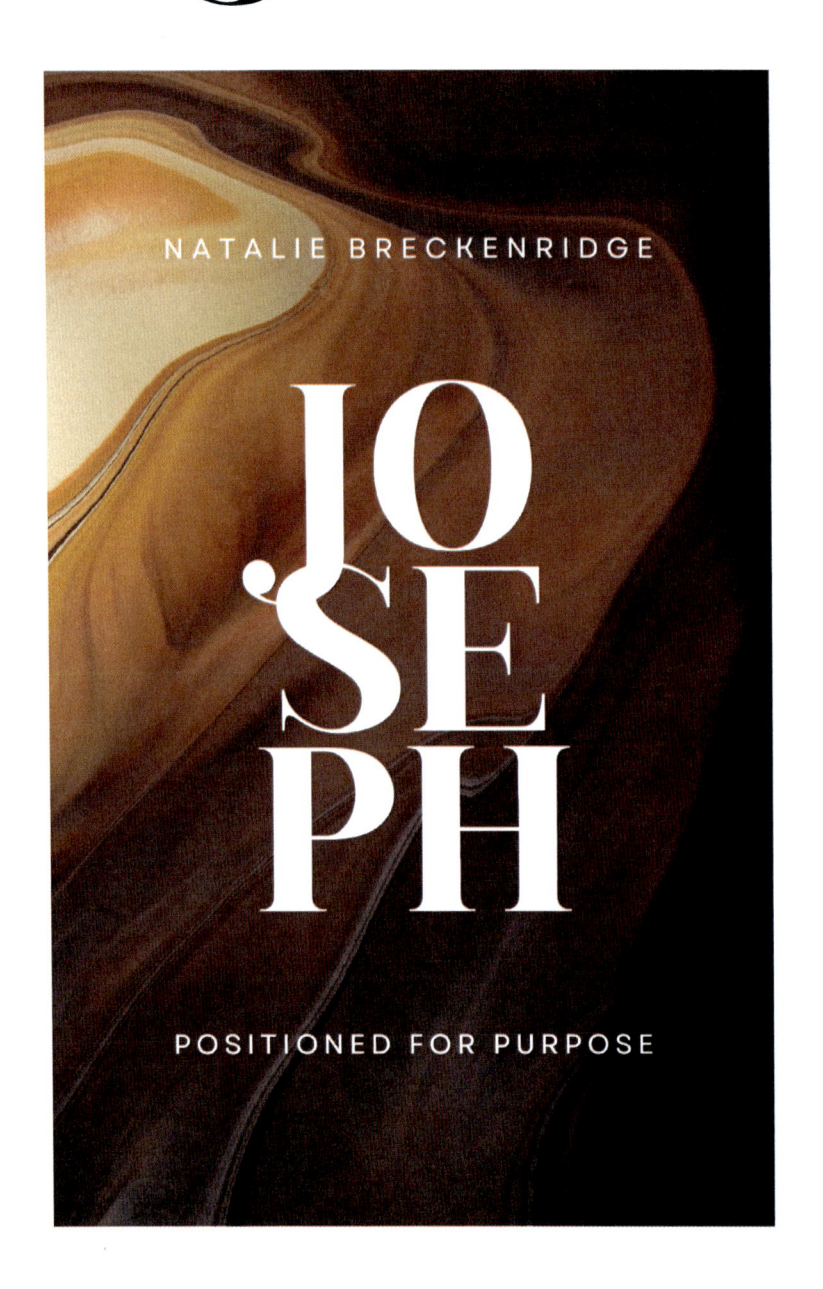

What if the moments we resisted the most were positioning us for purpose? True purpose. God purpose. The kind of purpose that exposes the plots of hell for what they are and renders them useless. The kind of purpose that marks your life and vindicates your soul from the "what if", "should've" and "could've" the disappointments that have kept you too long. If we are honest, most people do not fulfill their purpose. But God uses ALL things - all the pain & all the warfare. Get ready for the ride of a lifetime as we study the life and story of Joseph, the son of Jacob. No matter where you sit on the spectrum of your life, I am confident you will find yourself relating deeply to Joseph. It is time for you to be positioned for purpose!

Heal to Hear

Heal to Hear was written with one objective in mind: set God's people free from the pain lurking within. For far too long the people of God have been bound in their mind, in their ways of thinking and in their emotions, because simply put, they have no idea how to truly heal from the inside out. Equipped with a radical testimony of her own, Natalie takes on the serious task of walking believers through their own journey of finding peace within. She has truly created a work to 'set at liberty those who are oppressed.' Armed with both Heal to Hear and the Heal to Hear Journal, prepare yourself for a journey like none other. Get ready for beautiful, thought provoking change that will challenege you at your core.

Prayers for Real Women

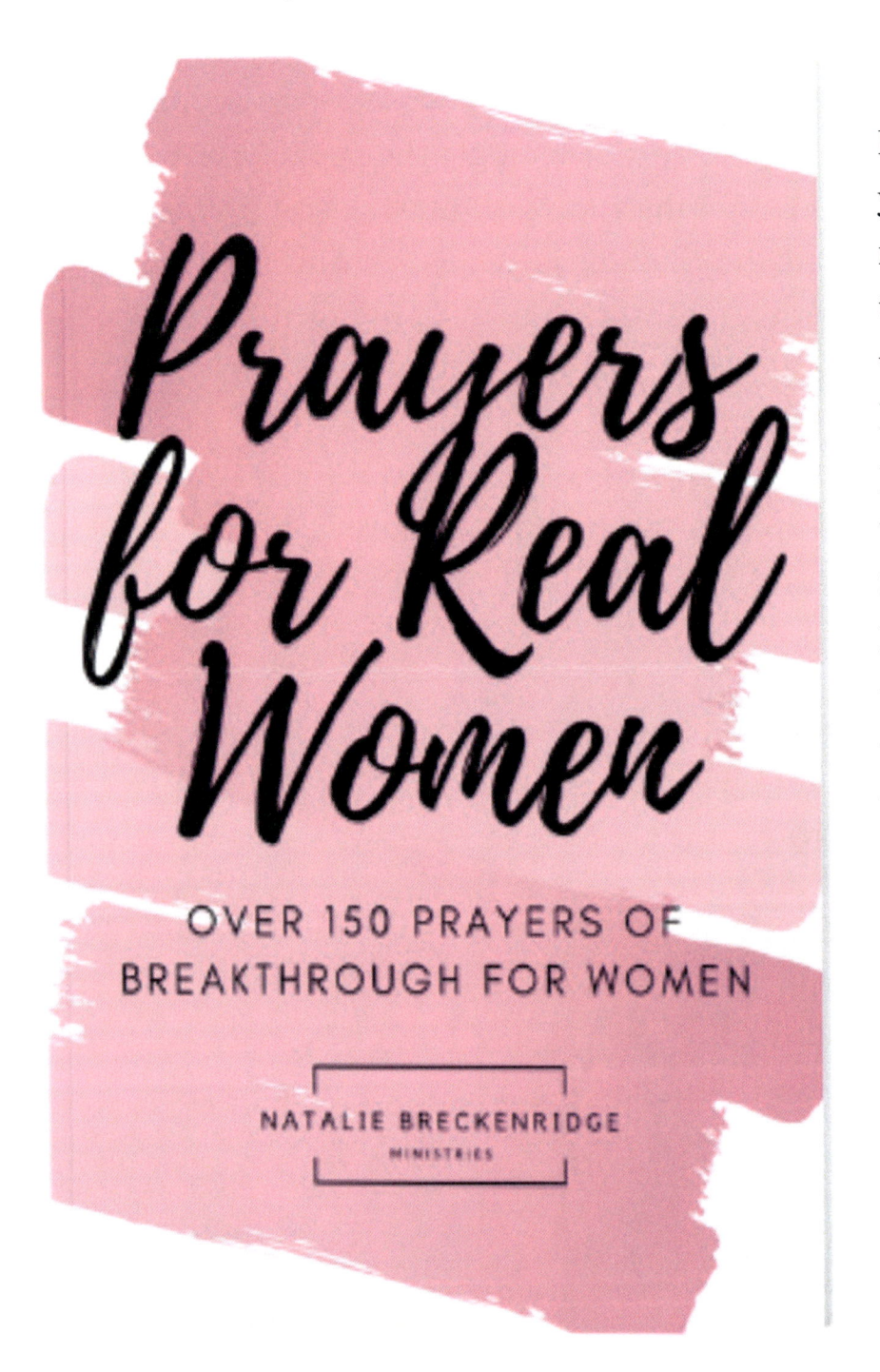

Do you sometimes find yourself knowing you need to pray, but have trouble finding the right words? Do you desire to learn to pray effective prayers and wage war with the promises in Scripture? Prayers for Real Women is a prayer tool for the modern woman. Topical prayers will help you discover prayer paths and practices that will make hell quake. Explore corresponding Bible scriptures that will deepen your understanding of prayer and how to pray the Word of God. If you're ready to go deeper in your prayer journey, Prayers for Real Women is a must have.

HOPLON
BY ZAC BRECKENRIDGE

AN APOSTOLIC STRATEGY

HOPLON

ACCESSING YOUR WEAPONS TO DELIVER SPIRITUAL WARFARE FROM HEAVENLY PLACES

ZAC BRECKENRIDGE

Hoplon, the Greek ὅπλον, can accurately be translated as weapon, tool, or instrument. In modern times, the church must become ever more aware that our battles cannot be wasted over physical diversions. Every movement sweeping our nation that is contrary to our Christian core values is not just a trend; it is a spiritual ploy to eradicate Christianity. The church has been cloaked with both heavenly authority and power as well as gifted with leadership to develop and implement those skills when necessary to stop the aggression of the enemy. However, we cannot enter into battle empty handed. May this book become a hoplon to spiritual warfare in modern times. May it become a training tool, an instrument to help us better understand our significance, and finally a hidden weapon in our arsenal by which we will expand the kingdom of God.